ANCIENT
MOSAICS

ROGER LING

PRINCETON UNIVERSITY PRESS

Copyright © Roger Ling 1998
Originally published in 1998 by British Museum Press
A division of The British Museum Company Ltd
46 Bloomsbury Street, London WC1B 3QQ

First published in North America in 1998 by
Princeton University Press
41 William Street, Princeton, NJ 08540

Roger Ling has asserted his right to be identified as
the Author of this Work

ISBN 0-691-00404-8
Library of Congress Catalog Card Number 98-066086

10   9   8   7   6   5   4   3   2   1

Designed and typeset in Monotype Bembo
by Martin Richards

Printed and bound in Spain
by Grafos S. A., Barcelona

HALF-TITLE PAGE *Hunted stag: detail of a tessera mosaic from Alexandria. The composition, in which a stag is dispatched by a pair of Erotes, recalls that of the stag-hunt in a pebble mosaic at Pella (fig. 12), but the introduction of tesserae indicates a later date. Alexandria, Graeco-Roman Museum.*

FRONTISPIECE *Head of a tiger. Detail of a mosaic in the courtyard of the House of the Dionysus, Delos. The tiger carried a winged spirit (Dionysus himself?) holding a thyrsus (Bacchic wand); the fine tesserae (only 1 to 2 mm square) and the black background are typical of Hellenistic pictorial mosaics. The panel formed the centrepiece of a white pavement with a border of wave-crest pattern in black. Late second or early first century BC.*

CONTENTS

1 INTRODUCTION

Mosaic is a bizarre art-form. The practice of setting thousands of small pieces of stone, terracotta, glass and the like into mortar or plaster requires a massive investment of time and labour. Where the result exploits the specific properties of the medium by juxtaposing pieces in different colours, there is some logic to it. But where all the pieces are in the same colour, or the mosaic uses carefully matched and graded colours to mimic the effect of a painting, the process seems a little absurd. The craftsman is going to great lengths to achieve something which can be done more cheaply and effectively in another medium. And yet such mosaics enjoyed enormous popularity in antiquity and the Middle Ages, with revivals of interest in later periods, notably the eighteenth and nineteenth centuries. The reason is, of course, that mosaics satisfied requirements that no painting could, especially in providing durability. Moreover, craftsmen came to apply their 'paintings in stone' in new roles and new arrangements, breaking away from the refined illusionism of wall- and panel-painters and often creating works of great originality. How they began to do this, and how their art evolved through the period of the ancient world, are the themes of the present book.

In antiquity, mosaics were designed exclusively to decorate architectural surfaces. In this context the term 'mosaic' is used primarily of techniques of insetting which employ pieces of standard sizes, not more than 4 or 5 cm across. Most characteristic is the mosaic which is made up of 'tesserae' – pieces of stone, glass or terracotta cut more or less to the shape of a cube. This was the form of mosaic chosen, *par excellence*, for the rendering of the geometric patterns, vegetal motifs and figure compositions used in pavements from the fourth century BC to the early Christian period; and it came increasingly to supplement and supplant painted decorations on walls and vaults. Another form of patchwork decoration which used larger pieces of stone or glass specially cut to shape (adopting the form of lozenges, squares, triangles, polygons, or indeed curvilinear shapes or parts of animal or human figures) is referred to as 'sectile work' (*opus sectile*) and will be mentioned from time to time in the present book, but it was far

1 *Example of* opus sectile: *tigress killing a bullock, from the Basilica of Junius Bassus in Rome (*AD *331). The use of pieces of cut stone in different colours to make geometric patterns in pavements goes back at least to the second century* BC. *Pictures made in this technique began rather later, probably during the first century* AD.

less common than tessellated mosaic, and, for all its prestige and costliness, its potential for complex and subtle effects was more restricted.

Ancient mosaics can be divided broadly, in correspondence with a distinction recognised in antiquity, into two main categories: those which decorated floors and those which decorated walls or vaults. The two categories eventually acquired different names, respectively *opus tessellatum* and *opus museum* or *musivum*; and, by the fourth century AD at least, the distinction had been reinforced by a difference of prestige, the wages paid to a wall- and vault-mosaicist (*musearius* or *musivarius*) being 20 per cent higher than those paid to a floor-mosaicist (*tessellarius* or *tesserarius*). This may reflect the greater dangers of working on walls and vaults (we know of at least one *musearius* who fell to his death while working 'high up'), but is probably mainly a condition of the greater visibility of walls and vaults, of the richer and more intractable materials (notably coloured glass) used on these surfaces, and of the greater prominence given there (eventually) to elaborate figural compositions. In addition, the lower status accorded to a surface over which people walked would naturally have militated against any privileging of the craft of the *tessellarius*, however skilled and time-consuming his work.

The surviving evidence overwhelmingly favours the work of the floor-mosaicist. This is partly an accident of preservation. The first part of a building to collapse, whether in a violent destruction or in a gradual process of dereliction, is the superstructure; the resulting debris in turn seals the pavements and protects them from the ravages of time and human interference. Disturbance by ploughing or the digging of foundations for new buildings may penetrate the upper layers of debris but leave the pavements largely or wholly unaffected. Where there has been no disturbance, mosaic pavements by reason of their durability are often recovered in pristine condition. Wall and vault mosaics, on the other hand, are rarely preserved, save in exceptional circumstances, for instance in the volcanic deposits which sealed the cities of Pompeii and Herculaneum in a kind of time-capsule, or in underground structures such as tombs which were similarly protected from the elements. In buildings which remained above ground, the wall and vault mosaics are invariably lost. This is true even in certain buildings which remain standing to the present day (for example, the so-called Baths of Mercury at Baiae, north-west of Naples), because the action of weathering has dislodged the tesserae from the mortar which held them (we can often detect the presence of mosaics only from their imprints in the vaults). It is not until the Christian period, with the magnificent series of mosaics on the walls and vaults of early churches, which have remained in use and thus in a good state of repair, that we have a large body of surviving material.

And yet the bias in favour of floor mosaics is not just a matter of preservation. It is clear that the use of mosaics on walls and vaults was much less common than in pavements. This was partly because of the greater cost of labour and materials in *opus musivum*, but was mainly a result of practical considerations. Given that there were social pressures to decorate pavements, this was naturally best achieved in a medium well suited to resist the wear and tear to which such surfaces were particularly exposed. Similar effects on walls and vaults, which were not subjected to such wear and tear, were safely and more cheaply left to the long-established medium of painting on plaster. This latter medium therefore continued to predominate over *opus musivum* in the vast majority of buildings. *Musivum* was used most frequently in buildings of high prestige, such as imperial palaces and, ultimately, Christian basilicas. It was also favoured, for both aesthetic and functional reasons, in contexts where water or water-vapour were present (see Chapter 7). Given its costliness, its use was often selective. It supplemented work in other media such as painting and stucco relief. One function was to produce mosaic panels which reproduced the 'old masters' of painting, and which, like those 'old masters', were set in painted walls.

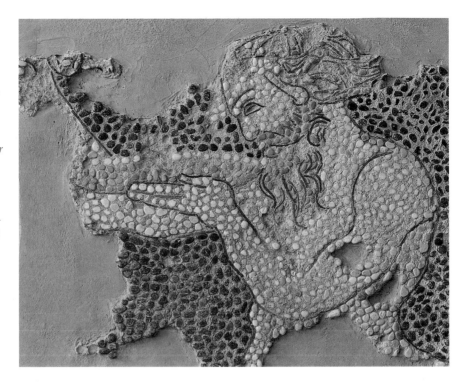

2 Detail of a pebble mosaic from Pella showing a facing pair of centaur and centauress, from the threshold of a large reception room. The light-on-dark effect and the use of leaden strips (elsewhere also of terracotta) to render linear detail are common in early Hellenistic pebble mosaics. They recall the colour balance and drawing technique of red-figure vase-painting. Last quarter of fourth century BC.

In view of the character of the evidence, most of this book will be taken up with floor mosaics. Here it is first necessary to stress that, while the favourite technique of antiquity (as of most later periods) was the tessera mosaic, there were other forms of mosaic paving which enjoyed a certain importance.

First among these is pebble mosaic, the original form of the medium. 2 This is a refined version of the cobbled surfaces used ubiquitously in more recent times for the paving of streets and pathways. With the aid of selected pebbles of different colours, mosaicists of Greek times were able to produce decorated pavements of extraordinary subtlety and variety, including not only abstract motifs but also vegetal ornaments and figure compositions. The pebble technique was soon superseded by tesserae for complex work; but plain or simply decorated pavements of pebbles occurred in certain contexts throughout antiquity. They are still found in the courtyards of modern houses in parts of the Aegean, for example on the islands of Cos and Rhodes.

A second type of mosaic is that formed of irregular stone chips. Again popular especially in the Greek period (fourth to second centuries BC), but found also in some of the late Republican (first century BC) pavements of Roman Italy, this technique absorbed the waste of sculptors' or masons' yards; its effect was similar to that of modern *terrazzo* paving.

3 *Pavement of* opus signinum *(mortar containing an aggregate of terracotta) with inset tesserae. This technique was popular from the second century* BC *to the first century* AD. *All the motifs shown in this pavement at Ampurias in Spain, datable to the first century* AD, *are favourites in this technique: a grid of lozenges, scattered 'rosettes' (four white tesserae round a single dark one), and a border of meander.*

3   A third form of mosaic, which may have originated in the Phoenician cities of North Africa and which was common in Sicily and Italy from the third or second centuries BC to the first century AD, employed patterns of isolated tesserae or chips of stone set in mortar. The mortar, which was generally mixed with an aggregate of ground-up terracotta obtained from pots or tiles, or occasionally (in volcanic areas) with crushed lava, to make it more damp-resistant, was the dominant element in the paving, but the tesserae, generally arranged in lines forming geometric figures, converted it from a purely functional surface into a decorative medium.

   This last example prompts a general comment. Many types of utilitarian pavement – not only those of mortar, but also those of stone flags or tiles (including fragments of tiles or pottery set on edge) – were as hard-wearing and waterproof as mosaics. It is an over-simplification, therefore, to claim that floor mosaics developed from a desire to make pavements more durable. Their principal function, as their rapid adoption of decorative treatments demonstrates, was to enhance the appearance of the spaces that contained them.

   It was this aesthetic role that promoted the success of tessera mosaic. The tesserae, particularly when cut small, could be tight-packed and arranged in juxtapositions of colour which produced astonishingly complex and subtle overall effects. Tiny pieces of different coloured materials, when viewed from a distance, would merge to create graduations and modulations of tone that mimicked the mixing of pigments on a traditional painter's panel.

Crucial to the colour effects employed in mosaics was the range of materials available to the craftsman. The commonest colours were those obtained from stone and terracotta. White and black (or grey) were provided by various kinds of limestone, or more rarely marble; black (or grey) could also be got from slate or volcanic basalt. Red, yellow and various hues from the same part of the spectrum could also be derived from natural stones, but were more easily supplied by terracotta. Frequently, pots or tiles of appropriate colours were cut up for the purpose. In Roman Britain a lustrous red was obtained from the red-gloss 'samian' pottery manufactured in various centres in Gaul. Colours that were not readily available in stone or terracotta had to be created in glass. This was particularly true of the richer tones of red, blue and green. Coloured glass tesserae were expensive and relatively difficult to obtain, and were not entirely suitable for pavements because of the risk of shattering, so tended to be used sparingly; they were much more common in wall and vault mosaic, where their reflective surfaces gave them a special aesthetic appeal.

For the techniques of preparing a mosaic pavement we have evidence from ancient writers, notably the Roman architect Vitruvius, and from the surviving archaeological material. Vitruvius, writing about 30-20 BC, was an idealist whose elaborate prescriptions are not reflected in many of the pavements that we can study. He recommended three preparatory layers: an initial layer of fine rubble (*statumen*), a layer of well-compacted mortar not less than three-quarters of a foot thick (*rudus*), and a layer of mortar

*4 Diagram of the make-up layers for a mosaic pavement, based on the instructions of the Roman architectural writer Vitruvius (*On Architecture *vii.1.3-4).*

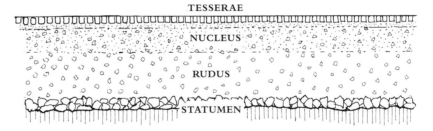

with an aggregate of terracotta not less than six inches thick (*nucleus*). In surviving pavements it is generally possible to discern only one or two preparatory layers of coarse mortar, totalling no more than two or three inches (5-8 cm) in thickness. Above this came a finer surface layer into which the tesserae were pressed. Since the laying of the mosaic might take a considerable time, this surface mortar was prepared fresh for each stage of the operation, just as in fresco painting areas of fresh plaster were applied for each new day's work.

What Vitruvius does not tell us is how the tesserae were prepared and how the decorative schemes were laid out. To make cubes of stone or

terracotta, the craftsman almost certainly sawed the raw material into sticks, then chipped off pieces with a hammer and chisel. Glass was chipped from specially moulded flat 'cakes'. The resulting tesserae would be graded by size and colour. No doubt, if there was enough work in one centre to keep a firm of mosaicists busy for a prolonged period, they would have stockpiled material in some form of depot. But many mosaicists were clearly itinerant (see Chapter 8) and would have done much of the preparation of raw materials on site. This is vividly demonstrated by the finding, in buildings where pavements were being laid, of heaps of tesserae, including half-worked specimens. Whether there was a central depot or tesserae were manufactured on the spot, craftsmen certainly encountered problems of demand and supply. Innumerable mosaics show examples of work in which a shortage of tesserae in the correct colour led to compromises, with supplies of one colour being eked out by the use of odd tesserae in a similar but different one or even by complete substitution of a different tone in part of the pavement. In this connection it is worth noting that, wherever possible, mosaicists salvaged and recycled material from redundant pavements: archaeologists have found examples both of mortar beddings from which tesserae have been systematically removed and of reused tesserae with traces of old mortar adhering to them.

Particularly interesting questions are raised by the choice and laying out of decorative schemes. The craftsmen certainly had pattern-books at their disposal, especially for figure compositions. No specimen survives, but that they existed is confirmed by an Egyptian papyrus of Greek times (third century BC) which refers to a pattern being sent from Alexandria to serve as a guide to a mosaicist laying a pavement at Philadelphia in the Fayum. It is difficult, in any case, to account for the close correspondences between mosaic figure scenes in far-flung corners of the Roman Empire without accepting that patterns of some form were in circulation. What form these took is unknown, but the limitations imposed by the size of available writing materials (wooden tablets and papyrus or parchment scrolls) dictate that they were small – perhaps annotated drawings like those that have survived for building plans. Collections of such drawings could have been assembled in scrolls like one being consulted by a figure in a relief from Sens in France which shows a firm of decorators at work.

There must, however, have been a good deal of flexibility in applying patterns to pavements. Though individual motifs recurred from pavement to pavement, the way in which they were combined, their size and proportion and their colouring constantly varied. We know hardly a pair of identical pavements from the whole of antiquity. An important factor was the variation in size and shape of the rooms that were to be paved. This

5 Head of Autumn in a pavement at Cirencester (Gloucestershire) in Britain, showing the use of glass tesserae (the deep red used for shading and for some of the fruit in Autumn's garland). At the bottom right there is an ancient repair carried out in opus signinum. *Late second century AD.*

made it difficult to lay down precise dimensions for the elements of the scheme. One way round the problem, illustrated by specifications for a circular pavement preserved in the Graeco-Egyptian papyrus just mentioned, was to divide the surface into concentric bands and friezes, most of which were given a specific width while one could be varied 'to fit'. More normally, however, the dimensions would have been dictated by the dimensions of the room. The surface was mechanically divided and subdivided using pegs and string to create a grid around which the pattern was constructed. The design, in other words, was reduced from the room rather than built up from preconceived measurements, and modern attempts to determine modules of design based upon specific multiples or fractions of ancient feet are generally unproductive.

Guide-lines for the main elements would be marked out in the underlying mortar. Examination of pavements where the surface has been damaged, or tesserae removed for display in a museum, has revealed several examples of such preliminary drawings, sometimes carried out in considerable detail, with (for example) the main lines indicated by incisions and subsidiary elements by painted lines in different colours. Once the tesserae were applied, any preliminary designs were naturally concealed. It is very likely that lines of tesserae were laid first along the guide-lines, and the infill executed afterwards; this was confirmed in the case of a Romano-British mosaic at Colchester (Essex) by the observation that the main dividing lines were in larger oblong tesserae which penetrated more deeply below the surface and had doubtless served as frames within which the subsidiary elements or figure work were executed. It seems that all mosaic work in antiquity was produced by the 'direct' method, that is setting the tesserae the right way up, rather than by the modern 'reverse' technique, which involves sticking tesserae face down on a cartoon drawn on cloth or the like, then turning the resultant panel over and setting it in position before peeling off the cloth. It is equally certain that ancient mosaicists did much of their work *in situ* rather than prefabricating parts separately before installing them. The only elements that are likely to have been prefabricated are detailed figure compositions. This certainly happened with many of the very finely made figure panels of Greek and early Roman times. Known by the Greek term *emblemata* (inserts), they were often laid, for ease of transport, on tiles or in stone or terracotta trays. Most of them were no doubt manufactured close at hand; but there is also evidence, both literary and archaeological, for examples being exported from one part of the Mediterranean to another. It is possible that even the larger pictorial compositions, such as the Alexander mosaic at Pompeii, were exported in this way, being shipped in pieces which were reassembled at their destination.

6 *Example of an imported* emblema *(inset panel): a scene from a play by the comic playwright Menander, found in Pompeii. This exquisitely worked piece (late second or early first century* BC) *is one of a pair of Menander illustrations recovered from the so-called Villa of Cicero; each is signed by Dioscurides of Samos, an island off the coast of Asia Minor. Naples, Archaeological Museum.*

But normally it was only isolated panels that were prepared in advance or bought ready-made from dealers, while the bulk of the pavement was laid on the spot.

As Vitruvius tells us, the tesserae were set with the aid of a rule or level. The rule, or any straight piece of wood, served as a template against which lines of tesserae could be adjusted. The level, an A-shaped device with a plumb-line suspended from its apex, was used to ensure that the pavement was horizontal (or, if necessary, slightly inclined). Other instruments, such as a set square or compasses, could be used to confirm the regularity of geometric shapes.

The final stages in laying a mosaic pavement, again recorded by Vitruvius, were rubbing down, smoothing and burnishing the surface. It was important that the surface should be perfectly smooth, because irregularities would result in tesserae being dislodged, which might lead to a gradual disintegration of the pavement. On walls, on the other hand, no such smoothing was required or desired. Part of a wall mosaic's aesthetic appeal was its irregular surface and the multiple reflections generated by the tiny variations of angle that the tesserae presented.

Before going on to consider the historical development of ancient mosaics, we may briefly summarise the main kinds of decorative systems that were employed. In pavements by far the commonest form of treatment was geometric. Motifs could range from simple chequerboards to complex compositions involving lozenges, octagons, hexagons, squares set diagonally, L-shapes, and roundels or other curvilinear shapes; arrangements could be continuous, that is with the same motifs endlessly repeated, or they could be centralised, that is organised in concentric bands or in radiating clusters round a central motif. Different parts of a room, especially a large one, might be treated in different fashion. The possibilities were legion. For a repertory of the main motifs and patterns the reader can refer to the excellent corpus of drawings by Richard Prudhomme published in Balmelle *et al.* (1985).

Less common and more prestigious were the various forms of figured mosaic. Earliest, and of enduring popularity in the eastern Mediterranean, came the self-contained scenes in panels, generally with a landscape or architectural setting, which reproduced the effect (and often the contents) of famous Greek paintings. These were treated as isolated showpieces, often at the centre of a pavement with a series of geometric or floral friezes surrounding and emphasising them. Later, in the Roman period, came spreading compositions in which figures occupied a free field covering much of the surface; background elements were omitted or reduced to isolated vignettes, so as not to pierce the floor with disconcerting illusions of spatial recession; the background was predominantly a neutral white, and the figures seemed to 'float' against it. In an early version of this style

7 (above) *Detail of a vault mosaic in a house at Ephesus. The mosaic, which belongs to the semi-dome of an apsidal fountain niche in a grand dining-room, shows the irregular surface characteristic of vault mosaics, with tesserae of glass which would reflect light from the water. The blue background is common on walls and vaults, rare on floors. About* AD 400.

8 (opposite) *Beast-hunt in the amphitheatre. Mosaic from a villa at Vallon (Fribourg) in Switzerland. The decorative formula in which figure motifs are distributed evenly, on neutral white backgrounds, within the compartments of an all-over geometric pattern is characteristic of mosaic pavements in the European provinces of the Roman Empire. Early third century* AD.

26-30 the sense of spatiality was further negated by rendering all figures in the form of black silhouettes. Finally, and most widespread among Roman mosaics, were schemes in which small, usually simple figure compositions

8 were set in separate fields of more or less equal importance within a basically geometric framework. This compartmental style, which to a large extent subordinated the figures to the decorative system, allowed for changes of orientation that reflected the likely movements of viewers within a room; it eventually became the standard form of figured pavement within the European provinces of the Roman Empire.

About wall and vault mosaics far less is known, but surviving fragments suggest that they generally followed the schemes of wall and vault decorations in other media, notably painting. Only in their colour schemes, and especially in the ultimate triumph of blue and gold backgrounds, did they exert a greater independence.

Details of wall and vault mosaics will be reserved for Chapter 7. In the meantime, we shall concentrate on pavements and discuss the development of their form and content in relation to their chronological and geographical contexts.

9 Example of a geometric mosaic in the baths at Djebel Oust (Tunisia). A rhythmic pattern of roundels and almond-shaped panels delineating concave-sided octagons is carried out predominantly in tones of yellow and green on a white ground.

2 THE GREEK PERIOD

The beginnings of ancient mosaic belong to the Greek period, and specifically to the late Classical and Hellenistic phases of Greek art, that is broadly to the last four centuries BC. There had been earlier manifestations of mosaic work of a different kind, notably the decoration of columns in Sumerian architecture of the third millennium BC with terracotta cones pushed in point-first; and pebble pavements with random patterns had appeared as early as the eighth century BC in Gordium, capital 10 of the native kingdom of Phrygia in Asia Minor. But the first disciplined patterns, and the first representations of figures and animals in mosaic, appeared around the late fifth and early fourth centuries BC in cities of the Greek world or within the Greek sphere of influence.

All the early examples are in pebble mosaic. Precisely how early, and in which part of the Greek world, the genre began, is uncertain, given the difficulties of establishing close dates for the early material. A pavement at Motya, a Phoenician city in western Sicily, used to be dated before the end of the fifth century; its technique seems typologically primitive, with patterns and animals rendered in white silhouette on an undifferentiated blue-black ground, and in pebbles of ill-assorted sizes which leave plenty of the mortar bedding exposed; but it is now thought that the actual date of this pavement should be brought forward and its primitive appearance ascribed to provincial workmanship.

Securely dated before the middle of the fourth century BC are the pebble mosaics of Olynthus, a Greek city on the northern shores of the Aegean which was destroyed by the Macedonians in 348 BC. Here a series of fine pavements from the dining-rooms of private houses in a suburb constructed during the last quarter of the fifth century BC show mytho- logical subjects, including the hero Bellerophon on the winged horse Pegasus killing the Chimaera, and the wine-god Dionysus in a chariot drawn by leopards. Each scene is set in a central field (in Bellerophon's case a roundel) enclosed by square friezes containing figures (Dionysus is surrounded by his retinue of satyrs and bacchantes) or bands of ornament (the meander, or Greek key, and the wave-crest, both destined to be great

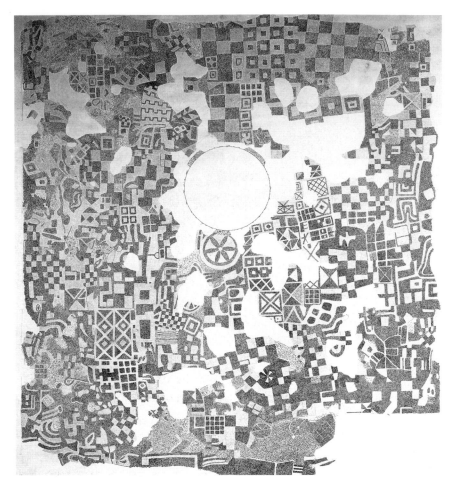

10 *Pebble mosaic at Gordium in Phrygia (central Asia Minor). This pavement of the eighth century BC is one of the earliest known patterned pavements in the mosaic technique; the patterns are, however, used in random arrangements rather than the ordered patterns of the earliest Greek mosaics three centuries later.*

favourites in mosaics, and stylised plant-scrolls). The patterned part of the pavement was skirted at the back and sides by slightly raised platforms of plain mortar on which the couches of the diners would have stood; the diners could thus have admired the floor decoration during their meal. There were further pebble pictures at the threshold of the room (animals attacking stags), and occasionally in a colonnade or antechamber which preceded it. Particularly noteworthy is the panel in the antechamber of the Dionysus dining-room, which shows Thetis and two of her sea-nymph sisters, each riding a sea-snake, bringing armour to her son Achilles.

All the Olynthus pavements, like that at Motya, have basically monochrome schemes of white and blue-black, but the pebbles are here more regular in size, producing relatively neat and disciplined effects. It is often suggested that the motifs and general design reflect the influence of textiles, and one can well believe that there is some truth in this; surviving fragments of Greek textiles, and more especially representations of them in

11 *Pavement of room 9 (dining-room) in the House of the Mosaics at Eretria (mid-fourth century BC). A few decades later than the mosaics of Olynthus, those of Eretria show similar motifs but with red and yellow pebbles in addition to white and black.*

other works of art, confirm that they used motifs seen in the Olynthian mosaics, notably the wave-crest border and the vegetal ornaments. Another source of inspiration may have been the red–figure vase-painting that dominated the Greek world during the fifth and fourth centuries BC. Not only do the Olynthus pavements include many of the same figure subjects and ornamental motifs as the vases, but their scheme of white figures on a black ground is analogous to the red-on-black used by vase-painters. It is easy to believe that craftsmen working in what was a new medium could have turned for ideas to an established one that had similar colour conventions.

The pavements from the Macedonian capital of Pella, datable probably to the last quarter of the fourth century BC, show considerable refinements in the pebble technique. The examples so far discovered come from two grand mansions which occupy whole city blocks and can thus be ascribed to leading members of the elite. They include all-over geometric patterns, notably a grid of alternating black and white lozenges which decorates a large anteroom; but the finest work is again to be found in figure panels decorating dining-rooms. Among the subjects represented are Dionysus riding a leopard, two huntsmen dispatching a lion, a similar pair of hunts- 12 men killing a stag – here with the aid of a dog – and a couple of episodes from Greek mythology: the battle of the Greeks and the Amazons, and the abduction of Helen by Theseus. As at Olynthus, further mosaic pictures decorated thresholds: a stag attacked by a griffin; a centaur and centauress. 2

12 *Pebble mosaic showing a stag hunt, Pella. The large scale, intricate detail and accomplished illusionism make this one of the masterpieces of the pebble technique. Last quarter of the fourth century* BC.

13 *Detail of a lion's head from a pebble mosaic depicting a lion-hunt at Pella. The figure is carried out in carefully graded pebbles, white for the body, pale blue and grey for muscles and shadows, yellow and brown for the hair, with strong outlines marked by strips of lead or terracotta.*

Some of these figure scenes are very large. The figures of the stag-hunt, for instance, are over life-size. At the same time, the modelling is more careful than at Olynthus, and the colours more varied. The developments in modelling are achieved with the aid of more careful grading 13 of the pebbles, smaller sizes being used for finer detail, and by packing them so tight as to conceal the mortar of the bedding. The basic colour scheme of white figures against a black background remains unaltered, but the inner detail of figures is modelled by lines of grey pebbles; there is also some red and yellow, in the hair for example; and one or two figures show hints of shadow. An additional refinement is the use of fine strips of lead and terracotta to mark strong dividing lines within figures, particularly for the genitals or where an arm passes across a torso. The use of inner modelling lines, and especially the distinction between strong lines in lead or terracotta and weaker ones in pebbles, again recalls the technique of red-figure vase-painting, which employed a relief and a matt line for similar differentiation; but in other respects the Pella mosaics represent a move towards panel- and wall-painting. Not only do they begin to display a greater range of colours (there is even some green in Dionysus' ivy-wreath), but some of the scenes suggest pictorial space by setting the figures on a ground surface indicated by brown, red and yellow pebbles. The pictorial impression is further enhanced, particularly in the stag-hunt, by subtle foreshortening and quite complicated overlapping – the dog over the stag, and the stag over the further leg of each huntsman.

The mosaics of Pella mark the high point of the pebble technique. It retained its popularity through the third century BC, and examples are known from various parts of the Mediterranean and even as far afield as Ai Khanoum in Afghanistan, the easternmost of the cities founded by Alexander the Great during his campaigns of conquest. The repertory includes not only mythological subjects and animal-hunts, but also floral and vegetal motifs, often (as in the borders of the Pella hunt panels) rendered with astonishing variety and virtuosity.

It was certainly the desire to achieve greater variety of colouring and to approximate more nearly to the appearance of painting that led to the invention, within the third century, of the tessera technique. Where this invention took place is no more certain than where pebble mosaics originated. A case has been argued for Sicily, but the balance of probability tilts in favour of sites in the eastern Mediterranean. This reflects the changing political and economic balance within the Hellenistic world. Alexander's conquests would have brought an initial flood of wealth to Macedonia, creating the climate in which the rich houses with pebble mosaics were built in Pella; but the growth of new Macedonian kingdoms in the East, and their success in exploiting the resources within their territories, led to a shift in economic power. The great centres of artistic patronage now lay east of the Aegean. It is therefore no surprise that two of the most important centres for the production of tessera mosaics were Alexandria in Egypt and Pergamum in north-west Asia Minor, the capitals of two of the richest Hellenistic kingdoms – kingdoms whose ruling dynasties (the Ptolemies in Egypt and the Attalids at Pergamum) were particularly noted for their patronage of the arts and literature.

Egypt was the first kingdom to be established, and, if any single centre was responsible for introducing the tessera technique, Alexandria can stake a strong claim. It has yielded a pair of hunt scenes akin to those at Pella, each enclosed by a frieze of exotic animals. The first mosaic, only partly preserved, is entirely in the pebble technique. The second, largely complete and showing a stag-hunt in which the huntsmen are winged love-gods (Erotes), is carried out mostly in tesserae, but with an admixture of pebbles and with continued use of the lead dividing strips used in pebble mosaics. This mixed technique, paralleled in mosaics from one or two other sites, can fairly be regarded as transitional. In Alexandria, at least, it had given way to mature tessera work by the early second century BC. Several panels of this date show a sophisticated mastery of the technique. A recently excavated panel from the royal quarter of the city depicts a surprisingly modern-looking dog squatting on its haunches next to an overturned vessel. Another found with it has a wrestling match between a white youth and a negro. Two panels from Thmuis in the Nile Delta each contain a female bust identifiable from its attributes as a personification of the city Alexandria, though perhaps subtly assimilated in its facial features to one of the queens of the Ptolemaic dynasty. One of these busts is especially fine. The tesserae are minute in scale (no more than one or two millimetres across), enabling the artist to produce subtle modulations of

half-title page

14

14 *Dog and overturned bronze vessel. This recently discovered emblema, found in the area of the royal palace at Alexandria, strengthens the claim of the Egyptian capital to be one of the leading centres of mosaic production in the Hellenistic period. The mastery of pictorial work in minute tesserae (opus vermiculatum) enables the artist to produce a highly realistic dog. Late third or early second century AD.*

colour and reflected highlights such as must have been present in the painted original from which the mosaic was presumably derived.

Pictorial mosaics in this highly sophisticated technique, the so-called *opus vermiculatum*, became characteristic of the Hellenistic period. They were regularly, like the pebble pictures of Pella, set as centrepieces in the pavement, with enclosing borders of subsidiary ornament, both vegetal and abstract, or with plain surrounds of tessellation or chip mosaic. Among the motifs used for the borders, the wave-crest and the meander (now frequently represented in perspective to imitate the relief meanders used in wall decoration) were retained from the repertory of pebble mosaics, while new favourites included the plait pattern, or chain guilloche, destined to enjoy continuing success in the pavements of Roman times.

The new style was avidly embraced by the kings of Pergamum. A pavement from a room in a part of the royal palace which is dated to the first half of the second century BC has unfortunately lost its central panel (evidently cut out by an art-dealer in Roman times), but its framing border, with a scroll of rich foliage inhabited by tiny Erotes and insects, can still be admired in the Pergamon Museum in Berlin. Also at Pergamum was laid the only pavement to be assigned to a named artist in a passage of ancient literature (Pliny, *Natural History* xxxvi, 184). The work of one Sosus,

15 *Mosaic of doves on a bowl, from Hadrian's Villa at Tivoli. The motif closely recalls Pliny's description of a panel laid in Pergamum by Sosus, the only mosaicist named in an ancient literary source. The black ground and illusionistic frame of bead and reel are both characteristic of Greek mosaics of the second century BC. Rome, Capitoline Museum.*

it consisted of a central picture of doves drinking from and preening themselves on a bowl, and a surround which depicted scattered refuse (lobsters' claws, fish-bones, nutshells and the like) from the dining-table, a design which earnt the pavement the sobriquet 'Unswept Room'. Nothing of it survives (unless a panel of doves on a bowl found in the villa of the Roman emperor Hadrian at Tivoli was the original centrepiece, imported from Pergamum), but the motifs were much imitated in mosaics of the Roman period.

The fact that Sosus' name was recorded by Pliny gives a hint of the status of mosaic pictures in the Hellenistic period. The skill of the workmanship required to translate paintings into such a cumbersome technique clearly evoked admiration and was treated by the artists themselves as a matter for pride. It is significant that several of the panels already considered carry the signatures of artists. The Pella stag-hunt was signed by Gnosis, the bust of Alexandria from Thmuis by Sophilos, and the missing centrepiece of the pavement from Pergamum in Berlin by Hephaistion (the dealer who took the rest of the panel left the signature, presumably because it was surplus, or even detrimental, to his purposes). These *pièces de résistance* clearly carried a prestige as works of art to which the mosaics of Roman times, most of which – in Italy at least – were anonymous, rarely aspired.

Alongside Alexandria and Pergamum, the two major eastern centres preserving examples of Hellenistic tessera mosaics are Rhodes and Delos.

Rhodes, strategically placed off the south-west coast of Asia Minor, was an independent state which derived its wealth primarily from trade. Delos, in the central Aegean, was raised to artificial prominence, eclipsing Rhodes, as a result of trading advantages conceded to it by the Romans in 166 BC; it became a major emporium, especially for the slave trade, until its destruction in 88 BC by Rome's enemy Mithridates VI of Pontus (a kingdom in Asia Minor). After a further attack by pirates in 69 BC it was progressively abandoned, and (unlike Rhodes) has remained unencumbered by any medieval or modern settlement.

Thanks to excavations by French archaeologists which have continued almost without interruption since the 1870s, Delos is the best-known of all Greek cities. Its residential quarters, containing the houses of the merchants and officials who settled there during its brief period of prosperity, have been extensively explored. They reveal that the art of mosaic had become more accessible to ordinary householders. Whereas the decorated mosaics of Olynthus and Pella had been confined mainly to dining-rooms, and those of Pella derived from houses of great splendour, at Delos mosaics are found in a variety of rooms (not only in dining-rooms but also in open-fronted recesses, upstairs rooms and courtyards) and in houses of comparatively modest dimensions. Mosaic, in other words, seems to have become not just a luxury restricted to the elite, but a decorative form available to a broad spectrum of middle- and upper-class patrons.

The range of mosaics found at Delos is as broad as the range of patrons. Central panels included not only figured *emblemata*, such as the Tritons (beings half-human and half-fish) from the House of the Tritons or the figure of Dionysus riding a leopard from the House of the Masks, but also motifs such as a rosette, a star or a wheel, or various abstract patterns, which present an equally valid viewpoint to spectators in different parts of a room. Where figure subjects were used, even in a dining-room, they were generally oriented for viewers entering the room; but this rule was not rigid. A depiction of an amphora (wine-jar) and palm-branch in the House of the Trident is designed to be seen from the back of the room. In all cases the figure motifs were isolated within patterned borders, or within areas of plain surfacing made of white tesserae or chip mosaic. Unusually elaborate is a circle-in-square pavement in the House of the Dolphins, in which the central roundel is framed by a plant-scroll and a perspectival meander between a pair of wave-crest borders set back to back, while the spandrels are occupied by pairs of dolphins ridden by tiny Erotes. The outer border is formed by a pattern of crenellations found earlier at Pergamum and probably ultimately derived from a motif in textiles.

With the Roman absorption of the Hellenistic world during the second and first centuries BC there was increasing influence from Greek art in Roman Italy. Many leading families of the Italian municipalities grew rich from trade in the eastern Mediterranean (there was a flourishing community of Italian merchants, for instance, on Delos) and these imported Greek works of art, or Greek artists, to glorify their cities or to beautify their homes. This meant not just bringing back or commissioning Greek sculptures, but also laying Greek-style mosaics. Some of the finest examples come from the cities buried by the eruption of Vesuvius in AD 79. From the House of the Faun at Pompeii, a private residence bigger even than the royal palace at Pergamum, we have a number of pictorial panels, many of them reproductions of familiar motifs: a winged Dionysiac spirit riding a tiger (found also at Delos), a cat attacking a hen, three doves pulling a necklace from a casket (a variant of Sosus' doves on a bowl), and

16 *Detail of the Alexander mosaic from the House of the Faun at Pompeii. This huge composition uses hundreds of thousands of minute tesserae to reproduce a late fourth-century BC painting commemorating Alexander the Great's victory over the Persian king Darius at the battle of Gaugamela. Here we see Darius, recognisable from his oriental hood and sleeves, looking back in terror and despair as the onslaught of Alexander's cavalry forces his chariot to turn in retreat. Second or early first century BC. Naples, Archaeological Museum.*

an extravaganza of marine fauna featuring a struggle between an octopus and a lobster. Most spectacular of all, located in an open recess (*exedra*) at the back of a colonnaded garden (peristyle), where it could be admired from outside, was the so-called Alexander mosaic, based on a painting of the late fourth century BC. This amazing composition, 2.70 m high and 5.12 m long, showed the climax of a battle between Alexander the Great and the Persian king Darius. The two protagonists, Alexander on horseback and Darius in his chariot, are surrounded by a mass of struggling figures. All the devices of illusionistic painting are here reproduced in mosaic: complicated overlapping, foreshortening, shading, highlights and cast shadows. Most striking are the representations of horses. One horse is shown in back view, going straight into the picture plane, while another, one of the chariot horses, is advancing in three-quarters view out of the background. The original painting was apparently rendered in a four-colour palette favoured by certain artists of the fourth century BC who prided themselves on being able to create sophisticated compositions by careful mixing of red, yellow, black and white pigments; but the mosaicist inevitably had to reproduce the mixed colours by grading and juxtaposing different-coloured tesserae. The tesserae used were only about two millimetres square, and it is estimated that the complete picture required, in all, some 1.5 million tesserae. Despite the apparent success of the project, close examination reveals a number of mistakes which suggest that details have been misplaced or misunderstood: a horse's hoof has become a rock, a Persian's head another, and various figures are incomplete. It used to be argued that this resulted from the assembling of many component parts prefabricated by the reverse technique, which prevents the craftsman from seeing his handiwork till it has been set in position (see Chapter 1), but a much more attractive argument, recently advanced by a German commentator, is that the pavement was originally laid somewhere in the East and was lifted and shipped in pieces to Italy, where mistakes occurred in the reassembling.

In support of the practice of importing mosaics from the East is a pair of mosaics from another house at Pompeii. Each shows a scene from the comedies of the Athenian playwright Menander, each is set in a marble tray for ease of transport, and each is signed by Dioscurides of Samos, an island in the eastern Aegean. The comedy scenes belong to a series known from reproductions elsewhere, both in mosaic and in painting. Most notable are the much inferior versions in a pair of late Roman mosaics at Mytilene on the island of Lesbos, again off the coast of Asia Minor, where there are twelve Menander illustrations, each labelled with the name of the play from which it derives. The Pompeii panels, showing figures wearing

17 *The so-called philosopher mosaic, found at Torre Annunziata, west of Pompeii. An informal group of seven bearded men in Greek dress, one of whom is pointing at a globe, is shown in an outdoor setting suggestive of the gymnasia or public gardens where philosophers held their discourses: a widely held view is that the scene depicts Plato and his disciples. Late second or early first century BC.*

18 Detail of the Nile mosaic at Palestrina. This remarkable pavement of the second century BC, which occupied the floor of an apsidal nymphaeum *(fountain)* in the style of a natural grotto, depicted the fauna, places and people of the Nile valley during the flood season. Here the central feature is a native reed hut with ibises on the roof and a herdsman and his cow at the water; below is a rower in a canoe.

theatrical masks and acting out their scenes on a shallow stage, are master-pieces of chiaroscuro, with the drapery tricked out in tiny tesserae of various hues. The technique is unmistakably Hellenistic, and one assumes that the artist was reproducing well-known paintings of Menander subjects.

That many mosaic pictures laid in Italian pavements were based on famous paintings is suggested by a pair of panels, one from near Pompeii and one from Sarsina in Umbria, showing a group of seven bearded 17 figures, one of whom is pointing out details on a globe. This has been variously interpreted as a depiction of the philosopher Plato and his acolytes, as an idealistic grouping of the Seven Sages of ancient Greece, or as a copy of a painting or relief displayed in Athens at the tomb of the rhetorician Isocrates. Whatever the correct interpretation, the nature of the subject-matter and the fact that it was repeated in more or less identical form in separate mosaics in different parts of Italy reinforce the idea that there was a common source, probably an old master painting, somewhere in the Hellenistic East.

One last pictorial mosaic that deserves comment is the Nile pavement
18 at Praeneste (modern Palestrina), 38 kilometres south-east of Rome.
Together with another, much less well-preserved, mosaic showing a grand
version of the marine 'aquarium' which inspired the panels of marine
fauna at Pompeii and elsewhere, it was laid in a complex of public buildings
dated to the late second century BC, and was doubtless a gift to his city by
a wealthy burgher who had enriched himself from trade in the East. The
subject is a great topographical map of the Nile in flood, with vignettes
illustrating the landscape, people and places through which it passed, from
the upper reaches in Ethiopia at the top to the Delta with Graeco-
Egyptian buildings at the bottom. There has, unfortunately, been much
restoration as a result of the vicissitudes suffered by the mosaic since its discovery in the sixteenth century, and it is sometimes difficult to determine
the original placing of the scenes or to reconstruct their precise form; but
the overall sweep of the composition can still be appreciated in the present
layout exhibited in the Barberini Palace in Palestrina, and the genuine
elements are sufficient to demonstrate that the artist had a remarkably
accurate knowledge of the topography and zoology of the Nile valley.
There can be little doubt that his source was a painting (or perhaps a
mosaic) in Alexandria or its vicinity; the pavement may even, like the
Alexander mosaic, have been directly imported from the East.

By the early first century BC tessera mosaic had gone as far as it could
go in the replication of illusionistic pictures. Varied colouring, modelling
by light and shade, perspective and foreshortening – all were successfully
conveyed by painstaking arrangements of thousands of tiny pieces of different kinds of stone. In some cases, such as the Alexander mosaic, the Nile
mosaic and its marine companion-piece, whole pavements were filled with
compositions of this kind; but the outlay of time and money required to
create such *chefs d'oeuvre* must have been enormous. It was more normal
to focus fine picture work within panels of manageable size, often only one
or two feet (30-60 cm) square, and to set them as framed panels surrounded by ornamental borders at the middle of the pavement. In this role they
to some extent usurped the place of painted pictures hanging on the walls.
Contemporary wall decorations were dominated by the so-called Masonry
Style, a fashion of working plaster in relief to imitate patterns of blockwork
or marble veneer, richly coloured but with no place for figure painting
except, occasionally, in narrow friezes at eye-level. Figure painting had, in
other words, moved down from the wall to the floor.

And yet the setting of illusionistic paintings in pavements could never
have been wholly satisfying. It would not have been easy to view them,
especially if they attained any size or came close to the walls of the room;

19 *Perspectival cubes:*
opus sectile *pavement
in the House of the Faun
at Pompeii. Patterns of
different-coloured
lozenges and the like, so
arranged as to produce
illusions of solid shapes
which advance or recede
in different ways
according to how the
viewer perceives them,
exerted great fascination
in Greek and Roman
times, especially in the
late Hellenistic period.*

unless the viewer stood directly above them, his perspective would always
have been distorted. There was also a problem of orientation. Most illusionistic pictures impose a specific viewing position, and Greek panel
mosaics were generally placed to be seen from the entrance of the room;
but this meant that viewers elsewhere in the room saw them from an
inappropriate angle. The diners in most Hellenistic dining-rooms, for
example, would have seen the pavement *emblema* either upside down or
from the sides. Furthermore, the very idea of using the pavement to display an illusionistic picture, with its capacity for opening a window into
another spatial dimension, is curiously out of keeping with the function of
a floor as the architectural element which should above all seem solid and
impenetrable.

For all these reasons there were many Hellenistic pavements in which
the central panel was given over to an abstract device such as a star or a
wheel (as noted above) which imposes no specific orientation and creates
no disturbing effects of recession. Another favourite device which has the
same effect, and which appeared both in the East and in Italy, was a
pattern of lozenges in three colours so arranged as to give an optical illusion of cubes in perspective – cubes which advance or recede depending   19
on how one looks at them. This could be carried out in tesserae, as happened on Delos, but it was certainly first invented in the sectile technique,
in which it is rendered at Pompeii. Such elements suggest a possible
dissatisfaction with the pictorial *emblema*, and they are the precursors of the
aesthetic shift which took place in Italy during the following period.

3 ROMAN ITALY

While the Greek cities of southern Italy and Sicily, and other cities around them, had been influenced by the emergence of pictorial mosaics of the Hellenistic type, there was another current of influence that shaped developments in Italy and the western Mediterranean. This was the tradition of mortar pavements (especially those of mortar containing an aggregate of terracotta, the so-called *opus signinum*) with inset stones. There is increasing evidence to suggest that such pavements were invented in the Phoenician city of Carthage in modern Tunisia, where isolated forerunners, including elements carried out in nearly regular tesserae, have been dated as early as the fourth century BC. Certainly earlier than the mid-third century are the pavements of Kerkouane, a short distance east along the North African coast, where fine *signinum* pavements are inset with small chips of marble or limestone or with more or less regular tesserae, either scattered at random or arranged in rows. Within one or two of these pavements tesserae were joined together to form good luck symbols, and at their edges there were sometimes continuous lines of tesserae acting as borders.

This kind of decoration was transmitted via Phoenician colonies to Sicily and southern Italy. It appeared, for example, alongside chip paving and pictorial mosaics executed in regular and irregular tesserae, at Morgantina in eastern Sicily (destroyed in 211 BC). At the same time, more diverse forms of non-pictorial pavement emerged in Carthage itself: mortar surfaced with fragments of limestone, mortar containing pieces of coloured terracotta, pavements with largish squares of terracotta interspersed with isolated cubes of limestone, even white tessera mosaic.

The expansion of the Romans through Italy and Sicily during the third century BC, and their wars with Carthage, ending ultimately in the destruction of that city in 146 BC, brought them, therefore, into contact not only with a pictorial mosaic tradition deriving from the Greek world but also with a tradition of mortar pavements enlivened with stones in an abstract style. It may have been such pavements that were condemned by the Roman statesman Cato in the phrase 'Punic pavements' as an example

20

20 *Detail of an* opus signinum *pavement with inset stones at Kerkouane (eastern Tunisia). This early example of a decorated pavement in the territory of the Phoenician city of Carthage, datable to the mid-third century BC, is a forerunner of the technique which became popular in Sicily and Italy during the second and first centuries BC. The emblem here represented, the so-called sign of Tanit, was a good-luck charm widely used in Carthaginian contexts.*

of Carthaginian luxury imported to Rome in the second century BC. They certainly had extensive influence within the cities of Italy during the second and first centuries BC. In Pompeii, for example, the pavements of *opus signinum* with outline patterns in tesserae were far more common than the better-known and more spectacular pavements in true mosaic.

During the first century BC, as the painted wall decorations of Roman Italy became more elaborate, such simple abstract floor decorations rapidly eclipsed the Greek-style pictorial mosaics. The wall decorations of the Masonry Style (the Italian version of which is normally known as the Pompeian First Style) now gave way to the Second Style, in which painters used illusionistic devices to suggest planes of architecture receding into a space – often immeasurable space – beyond the wall, and ultimately introduced a focal picture illustrating a scene from Greek myth, a rustic shrine, or the like. In the context of this new form of wall painting, with its *trompe l'oeil* effects and rich colouring, the use of similar effects in the floor would have been distracting if not overwhelming. More modest, space-denying treatments were clearly appropriate.

A limited use of polychrome *emblemata* can be traced for another couple of generations (and recurs occasionally in later times, for instance in Hadrian's Villa at Tivoli). As late as the third quarter of the century, the House of the Menander at Pompeii was provided with panels showing pygmies hunting crocodiles on the Nile (a favourite theme in a period of Egyptianising influence at Rome) and a satyr making advances to a bacchante. There was also a lingering interest in illusion-istic meanders and in schemes of coffering which reflected the wooden coffers of Hellenistic ceilings. A pavement from Teramo in eastern Italy bewilderingly turns the whole floor into an illusionistic ceiling formed by coffers containing rosettes, but opens the central part into a richly framed *emblema* showing a lion.

But such schemes rapidly lost ground. Even the *emblemata* in the House of the Menander were set in basically monochrome pavements, the first in a grid of intersecting black bands, the second in a plain white mosaic interrupted only by ornamental strips marking off the position of a pair of beds. Illusionistic coffering of the type that appeared

21

21 Nilotic scene (pygmies fishing) in the House of the Menander at Pompeii. Set in a black and white pavement of the 30s or 20s BC, this is a late example of the use of a pictorial emblema; *most Italian mosaics of the time favoured non-figural and geometric schemes. Egyptianising subjects were much in vogue in the years following Augustus' capture of Egypt in 30 BC.*

at Teramo and in a pavement from Via Ardeatina in Rome, now in the
Vatican Museum, gradually lost its illusionism and polychromy, until by the
time of the emperor Augustus (turn of the first centuries BC and AD) it had
been replaced by two-dimensional systems in black and white.

Alongside the lingering echoes of Hellenistic illusionism, the overwhelming majority of pavements now belonged to abstract styles born
from the western tradition. Lastingly popular, because of their visual sim-
plicity and their comparative cheapness, were the patterns formed by lines
of white tesserae set in *opus signinum* or, particularly in the cities buried by
Vesuvius, mortar with an aggregate of lava. The patterns favoured include
meanders, grids of lozenges, scale ornament (especially on thresholds or in
the vestibules of houses), and, for the focal position in a room, a large
roundel occupied by a star-like composition of lozenges, all enclosed
within a square border. Such pavements continued to be laid in the first
half of the first century AD, though often enriched with pieces of white
and coloured marble, presumably offcuts from the sectile pavements which
were then becoming increasingly fashionable: a single piece of marble was
set in the middle of each geometric shape.

Another fashion, though confined chiefly to the first half of the first
century BC, was for various forms of irregular stone paving which may
have been subsumed under the Greek term *lithostroton* ('strewn stone').
This was descended from the chip mosaic or irregular tessellation of the
Hellenistic period. In its simplest form small pieces of white limestone
were assembled like a refined form of 'crazy paving'. Alternatively, larger
pieces of white and coloured limestone were set in a background of regular or irregular tesserae, whether white or black. In one attractive variant,
these background tesserae were oblong in shape and set in pairs running
alternately parallel and perpendicular to the axis of the design so as to
create an effect of basket-weave. Such pavements were used, for example,
in the Villa of the Mysteries at Pompeii, where their two-dimensionality
and restraint provided a foil to the brightly coloured illusionistic architecture painted on the walls.

Of regular tessera mosaics, the simplest were plain white pavements
with no more than a border of one or two black bands. But increasingly
common were geometric schemes in black and white. These started with
two-dimensional versions of the motifs inherited from earlier polychrome
mosaics, such as the meander, but then developed a much broader repertoire of schemes and motifs, some of them borrowed from other media,
such as the stucco relief work which was now emerging as a major decorative art-form on ceilings and vaults. A particularly complex pavement
from the House of the Iliadic Shrine at Pompeii has its surface divided into

22 *Pavement from Via
Ardeatina, just south of
Rome, now in the
Vatican Museum
(Stanza di Eliodoro).
The pattern of square
and rectangular coffers is
based on the panelling of
wooden ceilings, though
the illusionistic style of
earlier versions has by
now (mid-first century
BC) given way to a
more conventional
treatment. The decoration
in the central area is
probably a fabrication of
the nineteenth century.*

large square fields, each of which is decorated with a different geometric pattern (based mainly on lozenges and squares but including one lozenge star within a roundel), all rendered in black outline on a white ground. Here again the wall paintings, representing human figures and a pair of elephants against a vivid red background, would have been offset by the two-dimensional, monochrome treatment of the floor.

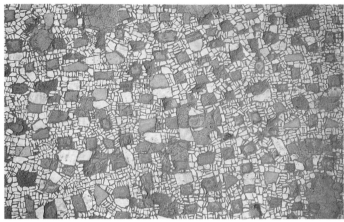

Such simple black and white geometric pavements dominated the mosaic art of Italy during the first centuries BC and AD, and, even in later times, they were often used as a cheap alternative for the new styles which came into vogue. The range of patterns included grids of octagons and hexagons, all-over meander, systems of large and small squares and oblongs with inset figures including roundels, concave-sided squares and lozenges. A long-lasting favourite, beginning in the time of Augustus and continuing through much of antiquity, has eight-lozenge stars so arranged as to enclose large square

43 panels and leave small tilted squares in the interstices. Such schemes were frequently enlivened with filling motifs, for instance triangles ranged one above the other, or point to point like an hourglass. Occasionally a geometric system acquired thematic value. A favourite theme was the labyrinth, where the viewer could trace his way from an entrance at the outside of the pattern along a constantly winding pathway to a central panel which often, in reference to the labyrinth of Cretan legend, showed a scene of Theseus killing the Minotaur. An early example appears in the early first-century BC pavement which gives its name to the House of the

24 Labyrinth at Pompeii. Another occasional theme was the city wall. Developing perhaps from the crenellated border which framed some Hellenistic mosaics, it was elaborated by schematic indications of ashlar masonry and by the addition of central gateways and corner towers to give the somewhat bizarre impression that the pavement was enclosed, like

30 a city, by defensive fortifications.

Within and alongside these schemes there were occasional representational elements. Stylised black plant-scrolls decorated thresholds or the borders which delimited the positions of beds in bedrooms or of the dining area in dining-rooms. Objects such as vases, dolphins and thunderbolts were set within panels. At Pompeii, a fierce guard-dog was occasionally

23 Detail of a pavement in the Villa of the Mysteries at Pompeii. This type of irregular mosaic, with larger pieces of white and coloured stones set in a background of small white chips (elsewhere regular tesserae, either white or black) is now often referred to by the Greek term lithostroton, *though it is far from certain that this is how the term was used in antiquity. Second quarter of first century BC.*

24 *Labyrinth mosaic, House of the Labyrinth at Pompeii (mid-first century* BC). *The central panel is an* emblema *showing Theseus killing the Minotaur, and, in accordance with a favourite Roman conceit, the surrounding pattern suggests the actual labyrinth through which Theseus had to find his way. Mid-first century* BC.

illustrated in the vestibule of a house, with the mosaic label CAVE CANEM ('beware of the dog') leaving no doubt as to its meaning. One dog was actually shown lying in front of a half-open door. In one or two cases there were more elaborate figure scenes, with the figures rendered in black silhouette. In the bath suite of the House of the Menander at Pompeii, for example, the pavement of the *caldarium* (hot room), dated to the third quarter of the first century BC, gives a foretaste of this style, with a black swimmer, a black fisherman harpooning a sea-snake, and further sea-creatures, all round a central flower set in a tondo. The blackness of the two human figures, together with that of the figure of a bath attendant in the entrance passage of the same room, is partly explained by the fact that they were evidently intended to represent negroes (the sea-creatures and the flower incorporate areas of colour, notably grey and red); but the mosaicist may also have seen positive merit in the choice of black silhouettes to decorate a floor. A century later, the pavement of the *apodyterium* (changing room) in the women's section of the City Baths at Herculaneum relied purely on black silhouettes: at the centre was a dominant figure of a Triton holding an oar, and accompanying him were an octopus, a squid, dolphins and, by a curious juxtaposition frequently found in Roman marine mosaics, a flying Cupid (Eros). These compositions were loose aggregations of isolated figures, but elsewhere more integrated scenes were attempted in the silhouette technique. A panel in the entrance passage of the House of the Boar at Pompeii – the panel

which gives the house its name – shows a wild boar at bay with hounds attacking it.

25 *Mosaic 'doormat' in the entrance of the so-called House of the Tragic Poet at Pompeii (before AD 79). The depiction of a dog straining at its leash served to callers as a warning, part humorous and part serious.*

Such silhouette figures are the basis of the style which came to dominate Italian mosaics of the second and early third centuries AD. Here we are fortunate to have an abundance of material from Rome itself and, more especially, from Ostia, the port of Rome at the mouth of the Tiber, which was extensively redeveloped under imperial patronage from the time of the emperor Trajan (AD 98-117) onwards. Thanks to the progressive abandonment of Ostia in late antiquity, and to its subsequent burial under encroaching sand-dunes, the structural remains of the city, complete with mosaic pavements, have been remarkably well preserved. Large areas have

been exposed since the early nineteenth century, and over 400 mosaics are now known.

Most of these mosaics conform to the general principle that the whole floor surface becomes a continuous field. A movement in this direction can already be observed in the cities of Vesuvius, where the marine mosaic in the House of the Menander at Pompeii retains an elaborate frame of meander and wave-crest but the later mosaic in the City Baths at Herculaneum has reduced the frame to a couple of black bands, allowing the figures to spread more freely within the room. In the second-century black and white figure mosaics this freedom becomes normal. The figures regularly cover the whole pavement apart from a black band or bands along the walls.

The introduction of the continuous white background is an important moment in the history of Roman floor mosaics. The old Hellenistic picture-*emblema* had evoked the idea of a window opened through the surface; it had treated the floor as a wall with a picture hung on it, and, since the picture invariably presented an illusion of space and setting, it was always a problematic concept. Putting the figures directly on a white ground meant that the whole floor surface became an illusionistic field; but the lack of landscape and the way in which the figures were distributed evenly across the surface negated the sense of recession and enabled the viewer to think of the decoration in merely conventional terms.

This reduction of the figures to conventional surface ornament was aided by further factors: notably the use of black silhouette and the changes of orientation from one figure to the next. The black silhouette remained dominant, even though white lines were introduced within it, first as a means of indicating overlaps or main body divisions, later for muscular and textural detail and even to suggest highlights. Already in the pavement in the Herculaneum baths, the central Triton has a vivid white highlight on his torso. In this particular instance the remaining detail is limited and simple; but in some of the second-century pavements at Ostia, such as those of the Baths of Neptune and the Baths of Buticosus, internal white lines proliferate, being used in a draughtsmanlike manner to suggest not only musculature, but also hair, creases of flesh and even (tentatively) shadow. By the early third century, in the Baths of Caracalla in Rome for example, the width of the white tesserae used for internal markings was varied so as to distinguish main dividing lines from less important details, while some lines were even tapered to a point. As a result, the white lines became more expressive, and the viewer would have found it easier to 'read' their meaning. In a sense, the technique had reverted back to the practices of the Pella pebble mosaics, where threads of lead or terracotta had marked out

26

27

26 *Pavement of the* caldarium *(hot room) in the baths of the House of the Menander at Pompeii. This mosaic of the 30s or 20s* BC *represents a half-way stage between the framed picture of Hellenistic pavements and the Italian black and white figure style. The human figures depicting negroes are black, but the sea-creatures and central plant include some colour (red and grey).*

27 *Pavement in the Baths of Neptune at Ostia (c. AD 140). A good example of the Italian fashion of decorating the floors of rooms in bath buildings with marine creatures (here with the sea-god Neptune driving four sea-horses at the centre) distributed freely in black silhouette on a white ground. The background is treated as water in which the creatures float, enabling changes of orientation which accommodate the changing positions of viewers.*

the main outlines of the figure, and lines of grey pebbles the muscles. But, all the same, the figures were still in 'negative'; the white lines on black figures were the reverse of the natural colour balance, and this served to weaken the viewer's sense of reality. However three-dimensional the modelling (and many of the mosaics exhibit a mastery of foreshortening), to conceive the figures as truly existing would have involved a certain suspension of disbelief.

The setting of figures at different angles within the pavement obviously counteracted any impression that the floor surface was a single spatial environment. It fragmented the decoration into isolated images which required different viewing positions and thus encouraged the spectator to move round. Wherever he stood within the room, this spectator would have seen one of more of the figures to good effect, but would have been aware that there were other figures which were best seen from another position. This made much better use of the floor surface than the Hellenistic *emblema*, which imposed a single optimum viewpoint. Naturally, in small rooms such as bedrooms or the offices of the Square of the Corporations at Ostia, where people would not have been expected to move around, the single-view subject was still employed. But in spaces of circulation, such as the large vaulted interiors of public bath buildings, the figures were oriented to favour the most logical viewing positions. Generally, the subject

28 *Insignia of a company of merchants or shipmasters, in the Square of the Corporations at Ostia (second or third century AD). Each of the offices in this square belonged to a company which traded into the port of Rome in the Imperial period; in front of their entrances were simple mosaics in the black-figure style symbolising their activities, rather like modern shop signs. Here two ships converge on Ostia's lighthouse; a dolphin symbolises the sea.*

29 Odysseus and the Sirens (soon after AD 123). This black and white pavement from Rome, now in the Vatican Museums (Braccio Nuovo), varies the formula of sea-creatures floating in black silhouette on a white ground by including a couple of Odysseus' maritime adventures, including (here) his encounter with the Sirens.

or subjects at the centre of the pavement were designed to be seen from the main entrance (or sometimes in baths, as in the *caldarium* of the Baths of Neptune at Ostia, from a principal bathing-pool) and those at the sides from the margins. These side figures could move continuously clockwise or counter-clockwise, or might converge to form facing groups at doorways. In baths, the standard use of marine motifs (sea-monsters, often with nymphs on their backs; Neptune driving a team of sea-horses; dolphins, sometimes ridden by Cupids; various fish and crustaceans) favours the multi-view formula because they are seen as floating; the white ground becomes an ambivalent space vaguely conceived as water. This works well; it is only where, as in several later mosaics, the craftsman chose to specify water by drawing parallel black lines that the changes of orientation lose credibility. More problematic in some respects are the subjects which belong on dry ground, for here the figures often have to be provided with short ground-lines, and sometimes cast shadows. In a large pavement in the Baths of the Cartdrivers (Cisiarii) at Ostia, dated about AD 120, the media 30 are inextricably confused. At the middle of the design, suspended as it were in mid-air, four *telamones* (architectural supports in the form of male figures) converge along the diagonals to bear the weight of a circuit of city walls which encloses a central drain; the motif was perhaps designed to 'reflect' a ceiling, with the *telamones* decorating the ribs of a groined cross-vault. Most of the remaining space is occupied by teams of muleteers and by a procession of marine creatures, the former in the bays between the *telamones*, the latter swimming clockwise round the outside. The whole composition is surrounded by a further circuit of city walls. The white background is more than ever ambiguous; it can be conceived as either land or sea, or from another perspective as the surface of a reflected vault, depending on which of the figures the viewer focuses upon.

30 *Pavement in the Baths of the Cartdrivers, Ostia (c. AD 120). The composition mixes various disparate elements: sea-creatures, mule-drawn carts, and* telamones *(male supporting figures) which look like 'reflections' of the decoration on a groined cross-vault. Round the edges of the floor runs a border imitating a city wall.*

Many further examples of the black and white style can be cited, such as the pavement from a villa at Tor Marancio, just south of Rome, where the marine repertory is given a Homeric slant by the incorporation of references to Odysseus' encounters with the Sirens and with Scylla. 29 Slightly different in form are those mosaics which overspread the white background with a geometric tracery of vegetal and floral motifs, amid which the usual black figures are dispersed at regular intervals. Here the spiralling tendrils confer a sense of pattern which 'absorbs' the figures and makes the changes of orientation seem less abrupt and less disturbing. Excellent examples survive at Ostia in the Tenement of Bacchus and Ariadne (c. AD 120-30) and in the Baths of the Seven Sages, where a great circular pavement laid about AD 130 flaunts an all-over composition of interweaving tendrils populated by huntsmen and animals. All-over vegetal compositions also came, as in the Hospitalia (guest rooms) of 31 Hadrian's Villa at Tivoli, to stand on their own, without figures, as an attractive variant upon the more abstract forms of geometric composition which had prevailed in the first century.

The black and white figure style was the major Italian contribution to the history of ancient mosaics. It showed an originality and boldness of conception which was lacking from contemporary wall-painting, whose practitioners continued to rework old formulae in an increasingly tired

31 *Black and white vegetal mosaic in the Hospitalia of Hadrian's Villa at Tivoli (AD 118-21). A series of identical rooms, each laid out with the plan of a triclinium (three-couch dining arrangement), is decorated with geometric patterns interpreted in vegetal and floral form, early examples of the so-called 'floral style' which became popular during the second and third centuries. The position of the couches is distinguished by plain geometric designs.*

fashion. Above all, it respected the function of the floor better than any previous figure mosaics since the experiments of the earliest pebble pavements. Its influence was felt in other parts of the Roman Empire, even in Greece; but its principal home remained Italy.

During the third century, coloured mosaic gradually supplanted the black and white style. Already in the Baths of Caracalla the black and white marine mosaics mentioned above shared the stage not just with black and white geometric mosaics but also with coloured compositions, including dynamic undulating patterns in black, white and purple in the Palaestrae (exercise courts). There was even at this time a revival of the perspectival patterns popular in Hellenistic mosaics. By the fourth century, coloured mosaics had won the day. The later mosaics of Roman Italy are more closely related to the pavements of the Roman provinces, especially the northern provinces and Africa. But before discussing these regions we must turn back to the East.

32 *Pavement with an overall meander pattern in the Palazzo dei Conservatori, Rome. The rendering of architectural motifs, such as the meander, in colours so arranged as to give the effect of volume is a popular theme of mosaics of the late Hellenistic period. Examples appear in Italy during the second and first centuries BC, and they seem to have enjoyed a revival in the late second and third centuries AD.*

4 THE ROMAN EAST

The eastern part of the Empire, that is the area corresponding to Greece, Asia Minor, the Levant, Egypt and Cyrenaica (the eastern part of present-day Libya), remained to a large extent Greek. The language most widely spoken was Greek, a fact which was recognised by its appearance alongside Latin in official inscriptions; and many aspects of civic organisation and social life retained the forms of the Hellenistic age. It is perhaps not surprising, therefore, that in parts of the East mosaic styles continued to reflect the Greek *emblema* tradition long after it was outmoded in Italy.

The region which provides the most vivid evidence for the continuing influence of Hellenistic mosaic is that focused on south-east Anatolia and the Levant – the Roman provinces of Cilicia, Syria, Palestine, Arabia and Cyprus. The fullest material comes from Antioch, the capital of Syria, now Antakya in modern Turkey. Here American excavations in the 1930s produced a series of mosaics (nearly 300 in all), in town houses, suburban villas, bath buildings and even mausolea, spanning the period from the second to the sixth centuries. These have been supplemented by discoveries in many other Near Eastern sites. Notable find-spots are Adana and Tarsus in Cilicia, Palmyra and Philippopolis (Chahba) in Syria, and Paphos in Cyprus.

Broadly speaking, the distinguishing characteristics of the mosaics of this region are a love of polychromy (the black and white style of Italy never gained acceptance), of illusionistic motifs inspired by architectural antecedents (meanders, oblong blocks, dentils and ceiling coffers in perspective), and of mythological or other figure scenes. The old Hellenistic formula of a central figure scene, rendered in pictorial manner with a realistic spatial setting which imposed a specific viewpoint, and enclosed by borders of geometric patterns or leaf-scrolls which threw it into greater prominence, remained fundamental. The chief differences are that the figure scenes tended to become larger, and sometimes to be multiplied, while the framing area was reduced in importance. Often the concentric borders of the Hellenistic style were substituted by an all-over network of geometric ornament based on intersecting circles, a diagonal grid or the like.

The mosaics from Antioch were unfortunately reburied or dispersed at the outbreak of the Second World War. Very few of them can be examined complete or even in one place. Fragments of the same pavement, not to mention different pavements within a building, are now divided between the museum in Antakya and various European and American museums. For an overall perspective of the discoveries and for details of their original layout and context we are dependent on a book which assembled and analysed the data 'after the event': Doro Levi's monumental *Antioch Mosaic Pavements*, written during the War and without access to the site or to most of the mosaics.

A good example of an early mosaic from Antioch is the pavement of the *triclinium* (three-couch dining-room) in the so-called Atrium House. Probably to be dated to a phase of restoration after an earthquake which struck the city in AD 115, it consisted of a T-shaped area containing panels with figure subjects, enclosed by a geometric border in the shape of the Greek letter pi (Π) for the diners' couches. The geometric part was not lifted, and probably no longer survives; the figure panels are now in four different museums. The three main figure scenes, arranged along the stem of the T, are derived from the standard mythological repertoire: the love-goddess Aphrodite sitting with her mortal beau, Adonis; the beauty contest

34 between the goddesses Hera, Aphrodite and Athena, judged by the shepherd Paris with the help of the messenger god Hermes; and a drinking

33 contest between Dionysus and the muscular man-become-god Heracles.

34 (right) *The judgment of Paris: detail from a pavement in the so-called Atrium House at Antioch. The seated Paris, wearing the cap of a Phrygian shepherd, receives advice from the messenger god Hermes as he tries to judge the beauty contest between Athena, Aphrodite and Hera. Paris, Louvre. Second quarter of the second century AD.*

33 (left) *Drinking contest between Heracles and Dionysus, part of the same pavement as the judgment of Paris panel (fig. 34). The sun-bronzed hero Heracles quaffs his wine-cup at the left, while the effeminate, pale-skinned Dionysus, reclining with his Bacchic wand (thyrsus) in his left hand, brandishes an empty wine-cup in his right. Though lacking the landscape of the Paris panel, this scene is no less sophisticated in its treatment of shadows and highlights. Worcester Art Museum, Worcester, Massachusetts.*

In the arms of the T were small panels containing isolated figures of a bacchante and a satyr. All these subjects are rendered with the colorism and illusionistic tricks associated with the pictorial *emblemata* of Hellenistic times (though these were not technically *emblemata*, since there is no sign that they were executed separately and inserted in the pavement). The three main scenes, in particular, reproduce elaborate effects of cascading drapery, highlighted metalwork and sun-bronzed flesh, and all set the figures in a spatial environment, whether indoors or outdoors. This pictorial treatment, and the luxuriant scrolls on black backgrounds which framed the two largest panels, are features firmly rooted within the Hellenistic tradition; but the size of the pictures, their juxtaposition to form a series, and the general T-shaped arrangement are all characteristic of the Roman period. The other border motifs include both Hellenistic favourites such as the wave-crest and others that, while not unknown in Hellenistic mosaics, are more common in Roman times — the two-dimensional meander, stepped pyramids and (the most ubiquitous of all Roman borders) the simple two-strand guilloche.

Another *triclinium* mosaic of similar T form and similar date comes from the House of the Calendar. Here the cross-bar of the T featured a large panel with the sea-deities Oceanus and Tethys surrounded by fish and marine plants, while its stem, here far fatter than in the Atrium House, contained one of the oldest representations of the Roman calendar, showing personifications of the twelve months arranged in a great wheel-like circle round a central medallion (now destroyed), with busts of the Seasons in the angles. Notable in this pavement is a polychrome border of square and oblong panels containing inset lozenges, rendered in pink, brown, yellow, grey and white. The bright colouring of these panels and of the floral motifs within them, together with their broad frames and changes of colouring which hint at perspective, call to mind the imitation ceiling coffers of the late Hellenistic period; but the pavement as a whole is unmistakably a product of the Roman age. The extent of the figure work in relation to the floor area is a far cry from the small focal panels of Delos and other Hellenistic sites. Among the new elements destined to enjoy lasting popularity in Imperial mosaic is the so-called 'undulating ribbon' which appears in the inner border of the marine panel. This motif, which exploits carefully graded tesserae of different colours — here white, grey, pink and red — to suggest a sinuous curvature in three dimensions, appealed

35

35 *Oceanus reclining amid marine fauna, from the House of the Calendar at Antioch (second century AD). This figure, characterised by the ship's rudder which he holds in his right hand, appeared in one arm of the T-shaped area within a triclinium mosaic whilst Tethys, Oceanus' consort, was depicted in the other. In the border (just visible at the top) there is an early example of the 'undulating ribbon'. Antakya Museum, Turkey.*

36 *Drinking contest between Heracles and Dionysus, from the House of the Drinking Contest at Seleucia, the port of Antioch. This is a later version of the same subject depicted in fig. 33; it belongs to a group of Antiochene pavements of the early third century AD in which illusionistic pictures are set in architectural structures apparently derived from wall paintings. Princeton University, Art Museum.*

particularly to the taste of mosaicists in the East for illusionism and technical virtuosity.

Polychromy and illusionism continued to dominate in later periods. The Severan age, which spans the last years of the second and the first third of the third century, saw a fashion for ever more baroque effects. A small group of mosaics set mythological figure scenes, including another version of the drinking contest between Dionysus and Heracles, within architectural frames perhaps inspired by the columnar backdrops of Roman theatre stages. This device, clearly borrowed from wall-painting, looks decidedly odd in a picture laid on a floor, particularly when the framing columns and entablature are indicated with strong *trompe l'oeil* recession within a pavement which is otherwise covered by an all-over network of geometric ornament (in the House of the Drinking Contest a coloured version of the eight-star lozenge pattern much favoured in the black and white style of Italy and the West). There are few clearer examples of the problematic effects of 'opening' the floor with illusionistic pictures which both contradict the architectonic function of the floor surface and impose a very specific viewpoint on the observer.

36

A general trend of the mosaics of Antioch, and of those in other eastern cities, was the increasing use of personifications. Many of these were (or were destined to be) established types in the repertoire of the decorative arts throughout the Roman Empire. The four Seasons, and the months of the year, have already been mentioned. Geographical personifications, too, a familiar motif in ancient art, made regular appearances in eastern mosaics. At Seleucia, the port of Antioch, there is a pavement with a central picture including a seated female figure personifying Cilicia and corner medallions containing busts of river-gods (only Tigris and Pyramus survive). At Mas'udiye on the east bank of the Euphrates, a region newly acquired for the Empire by Septimius Severus, a mosaic dated by an inscription to AD 227–8 shows the river Euphrates, a bearded male figure with a crown of reeds, reclining between standing female personifications of Syria and Mesopotamia.

37 *Apolausis mosaic in the so-called Bath of Apolausis, near Antioch (c. AD 400). The bust of Apolausis (Enjoyment) is the only figural element in an otherwise purely geometric composition; she presumably symbolises the condition to which bathers should aspire. Personifications of abstract concepts became popular in eastern cities during the late second and third centuries AD. A label ensures that the viewer knows which concept is intended. The mosaic is now in the Dumbarton Oaks Research Collection and Library, Washington, D.C.*

Less familiar are the more strictly abstract concepts, such as Bios (Life), Tryphe (Luxury), Amerimnia (Security), Gethosyne (Joy), Euandria (Manliness), Dynamis (Power), Ktisis (Foundation), Ananeosis (Renewal), Soteria (Safety), Apolausis (Enjoyment), Agora (Abundance) and Eukarpia (Fertility). Such personified ideas are most frequently shown in the form of isolated busts. In some cases one of them forms the sole figural subject in a room, occupying a panel surrounded by geometric ornament. The idea may here have conveyed a moral message to users of the room, symbolising a virtue to aspire to or a desirable condition to attain; at the same time it must have served as a convenient marker after which the room could have been named: e.g. Apolausis Room, Soteria Room or Ananeosis Room. 37

But the personifications did not necessarily appear in isolation. Sometimes, especially from the third century onwards, they came together in allegorical figure scenes – scenes which testify to the increasing academicism of the Imperial age and to a particular preoccupation of eastern householders with philosophical speculation. A famous example groups a figure of Aion (Eternity) with the three Chronoi (Stages of Time), namely Past, Present and Future: this clearly illustrates a theme debated in the third-century Neo-Platonic school of philosophy. A more worldly grouping shows Opora (personification of Autumn) reclining with Agros (the Field) while Oinos (Wine, represented as a Silenus, one of the elderly spirits in Dionysus' retinue) serves them drinks. At Philippopolis, in an obvious allegory of the role of agriculture in promoting prosperity, Earth and the Seasons are seen paying homage to two divinities of fertility accompanied by Wealth. Also at Philippopolis, a scene of a seated Euteknia 38 with Dikaiosyne and Philosophia standing in attendance both glorifies the ideal of Eugenics and symbolises the importance of Justice and Philosophy in a child's upbringing.

38 *Euteknia (symbolising the boon of good children) seated between Dikaiosyne (Justice) and Philosophia (Philosophy): mosaic panel from Philippopolis (Chahba) in Syria. A good example of the allegorical scenes with abstract ideas in personified form which became popular in the East during the third century AD. Damascus Museum.*

Such abstract images, and indeed many of the geographical personifications too (given that conventional attributes were rarely adequate to distinguish one region or one river from another), tended to be so obscure as to require that the figures were labelled. Labels became increasingly frequent in eastern mosaics, as also in eastern wall paintings, from the third century onwards. They inaugurated a fashion which spread also to representations of mythical subjects. Since many of these subjects had hitherto been depicted without labels, and since it usually remained possible for the narrative to be identified from visual signifiers within the scenes, we must assume that the practice of labelling was largely conventional. However, in some early examples there is an element of selectivity which implies that the mosaicists or their patrons felt the need to assist viewers with the less well-known subjects whilst assuming that they could cope with the more familiar ones. Thus, in a sequence of four scenes in the portico of the House of Dionysus at Paphos, two — the love stories of Poseidon (Neptune) and Amymone and of Apollo and Daphne — were regarded as sufficiently well known (and easy to recognise from iconographic clues within the composition) for all inscriptions to be omitted; but the stories of Pyramus and Thisbe and of Dionysus and Icarius, being slightly more recondite, had to have the chief protagonists labelled. There was clearly an awareness of the problems of communicating meaning to some of the visitors to the house.

89

In the fourth century labels were ubiquitous. This is demonstrated by further mosaics at Paphos. A roundel depicting the killing by Theseus of the Minotaur, though not obscure in meaning, has labels attached to all the figures: Theseus and the Minotaur themselves, Theseus' lover Ariadne, a reclining male figure symbolising the Labyrinth, and a personification of Crete, unmistakable because of her mural crown, a conventional attribute of cities and provinces. An even more striking example is the great *triclinium* mosaic of the House of Aion, excavated in the 1980s, where no fewer than

39 *The satyr Marsyas is taken away by a pair of Scythian slaves to be flayed alive after losing his musical contest with the god Apollo (seated at the right): Marsyas' young pupil Olympus pleads with the god to show mercy. One of a series of five panels with multi-figure subjects from Greek mythology arranged in the central part of a dining-room pavement in the House of Aion at Paphos, Cyprus. Second quarter of the fourth century* AD.

five multi-figure compositions were laid out in three tiers to invite the scrutiny of guests as they entered the room. At the top come two panels representing respectively the story of Leda's seduction by Zeus in the guise of a swan and the handing over of the infant Dionysus to be reared by the nymphs of Mount Nysa; in the middle, occupying the full length of the frieze, is a depiction of the beauty contest between Cassiopeia and the Nereids; at the bottom, once more in separate panels, the young Dionysus rides in triumph on a chariot drawn by centaurs, and Marsyas is taken off to be flayed alive after his disastrous musical challenge to the god Apollo. These five scenes contain, in total, nearly fifty figures; and virtually every one of them, whether readily recognisable or not, is labelled. In the Marsyas panel, the myth was such a familiar one, and the figures so clearly characterised, that the labelling of the figures seems almost redundant. Only Plane (Error) in the background, apparently a personification of the delusion which had led Marsyas to think that he could win a contest with Apollo, might have posed problems of identification without a label. In the other panels there are more figures for which labels are necessary. In the Leda scene, for instance, while the combination of a nude female figure and a swan leaves the subject and the identity of the two main protagonists beyond doubt, and while the personifications of Lacedaemonia and the River Eurotas on the right might have been recognisable from their sex and attributes and from a knowledge of where the event took place, the identification of the three female figures on the left, labelled as 'Lakaine' (Lacedaemonian women), would hardly have been secure without the label. In earlier periods artists would rarely have used labels, even where figures were subordinate or obscure; but in these fourth-century mosaics they have become *de rigueur*.

In regard to ornament a major development in eastern mosaics was the introduction of the so-called 'rainbow style'. Established by the end of the third century, and at the height of its popularity during the fourth and fifth, this style achieved popularity also in Africa and the West, but appealed particularly to the eastern taste for colour and virtuosity. In effect it rejected the traditional approach of mosaicists, which was to construct ornament in linear terms, using rows of tesserae to define the contours of each constituent element, then filling the interior with further parallel rows. Instead, it substituted a method of laying tesserae point to point, with colours changing in diagonal sequence, so as to produce a kaleidoscopic effect which exploited rather than concealed the tessera technique. For the first time craftsmen cast off the shackles of the pictorial approach by which they had been dominated for six or seven centuries and began to show an awareness of the specifically mosaicistic possibilities of their medium.

The new method was applied in various decorative forms. A favourite was the 'rainbow cable', in which colours were graded to produce the appearance of a convex band, which was then used to frame individual panels or to build up whole decorative schemes. More popular still were areas infilled with continuous patterns (zigzags, tilted squares or simple oblique lines) rendered in tesserae set point to point, again in graded hues. Such patterns produced a dazzling display of colour more truly akin to the effects of pointillism than any other style in ancient mosaic. The technique was, however, reserved for ornament: figure work continued to be executed in the traditional contour-based style. Much of the interest of the fourth-century mosaics of Antioch and other eastern sites consists in the

juxtaposition of figure scenes in the old manner and pattern-work in the new. In the House of Menander at Antioch, for instance, a panel depicting the myth of Apollo and Daphne in standard pictorial terms is set between a pair of rainbow mats, one containing a decoration of zigzags arranged symmetrically on either side of three squares, the other a continuous series of zigzags. In some later pavements large tracts of ornament were rendered in the rainbow style, with forms dissolved into impressionistic plays of light and colour. The fifth-century mosaic of Ananeosis, also at Antioch, uses the technique so extensively that it presents the appearance of a woven textile.

Mosaic figure work in the East remained faithful to its Hellenistic roots at least down to the end of the fourth century. Some scenes reduced the importance of the setting, or even replaced it with a neutral white ground of a type favoured in Africa and the West: the version of Orpheus charming the animals from Adana, for example, sets the different elements of the composition on little ground-lines within an otherwise undifferentiated white field, in striking contrast with the more realistic spatial environment, with the animals among rocks, of the version from nearby Tarsus. On the whole, however, eastern figure mosaics of the fourth century preserved a sense of volume and spatial recession which seems astonishing at such a

40 *Mosaic in the House of Menander at Daphne, outside Antioch: Apollo and Daphne between a pair of 'rainbow' mats. The conventional contour-based technique of the figure scene contrasts with the new style of the abstract ornament, in which tesserae of different colours are set point to point to produce kaleidoscopic effects.*

late date. It was not till the fifth century, after the emperor Theodosius had delivered the *coup de grâce* to pagan ideals, that the old 'Classical' style passed from fashion, to be replaced by a new style and by new priorities in the choice of subject-matter (see Chapter 7).

While the mosaics of the Levantine provinces retained a broadly Hellenistic treatment throughout the Imperial period, those of European Greece and the western parts of Anatolia seem to have been strongly influenced by the styles and themes of Italy and the West. Recent research has suggested that economic factors here produced a decisive break with the Hellenistic tradition. The Mithridatic Wars of the early first century BC and the subsequent civil wars of the late Republic, fought largely on Greek soil and financed largely by Greek contributions, resulted in a period of economic stagnation which ruined the mosaic industry. The demand for new mosaics came to a stop, and workshops were forced to disband for lack of commissions. The demand revived with an upturn in economic conditions in the second century AD, but at this point craftsmen looked to

41 *Orpheus and the beasts, from Adana in Cilicia (now Turkey), c. AD 300. Unusually for an eastern figure scene, this version renounces a realistic spatial setting in favour of an African-style composition of isolated figures at different levels on a white ground. Adana Museum.*

the West for inspiration, and the new wave of mosaics adopted the black and white geometric and silhouette figure styles of Italy. When polychromy and illusionism returned in the third century, it was as part of a general movement which affected Italy too.

The only other place in the East where the Italian style gained any sort of foothold was Judaea, but this was for a brief period and in a special context. The pavements of the fortress-palace of Herod the Great at Masada, built in the 30s BC, include some that show Italian influence of a kind which implies immigrant craftsmen or, at the very least, deliberate

42

imitation. Two of them have a network of black hexagons on a white ground, a specifically Italian motif unknown elsewhere in the East. However, the art and architecture of Herod, who had spent some time as a refugee in Rome, demonstrate other close links with Italy and may be explained by the particular preferences of a philo-Roman patron. Moreover, Herod's commitment to Italian ideas was not unreserved: other mosaics in his palaces employ the centralised schemes and rich colouring of the Hellenistic style. The few Italian-style mosaics are the exception that prove the rule: that the main current of mosaic production in the eastern Mediterranean during Imperial times was one that evolved directly, with little outside influence, from the traditions of the Hellenistic age.

5 THE ROMAN NORTH-WEST

Unlike the provinces of the eastern half of the Empire, the northern and western provinces (Gaul, Germany, Britain, Spain and the provinces of the Alps and the Danube frontier) had no native tradition of mosaic production before they became part of the Empire. Only the Greek and Phoenician colonies along the Mediterranean coasts would have had the degree of urban culture, and the awareness of traditions of interior decoration, required for the commissioning of mosaics. But, apart from some tantalising remains of pebble mosaics at Cástulo in southern Spain which may be as early as the fifth and fourth centuries BC, there are few decorated pavements before the spread of Roman power, first along the Mediterranean shores of Spain and Gaul during the second and early first centuries BC, then, with the conquests of Caesar and Augustus in the first century, to the rest of western Europe apart from Britain (added during the first century AD).

Even after the arrival of the Romans, decorated pavements were at first confined largely to the Mediterranean coasts. The early examples represent the Punic-Italian tradition of patterns of tesserae set in *opus signinum*. The Greek port of Emporion (Ampurias) in Catalonia has yielded pavements 3 in this technique with lozenge grids and roundels containing radiating patterns of lozenges, all framed by bands of swastika meander. Further examples come from Glanum (Saint-Rémy-de-Provence), long exposed to the cultural influence of the Greeks of nearby Massalia (Marseille).

It was during the first century AD that the 'Romanisation' of the conquered territories brought a gradual spread of mosaic (along with other Graeco-Roman art-forms, such as wall-painting, large-scale stone sculpture and monumental architecture) through western Europe. Not surprisingly, the stylistic links are with the Italian rather than the eastern tradition. Numerous sites provide evidence of black and white geometric pavements like those which prevailed in Roman Italy in the early Imperial period. At Ampurias, the excavated houses of the Roman quarter have yielded a fine range of mosaics in this style, including grids of octagons, four-point stars and hexagons, lozenges and swastikas, and eight-lozenge stars enclosing 43

squares. At Fréjus (Forum Julii) in Provence, one pavement has a pattern of black and white chequers carrying pairs of triangles arranged point to point in hourglass fashion, while another has the composition of lozenge-stars and squares again, the squares here containing different filling patterns and motifs. These examples are still from the Mediterranean shores, but one of the fullest series, dated around AD 75, is that of a villa at Fishbourne (Sussex) in Britain. A great variety of black and white schemes, including the lozenge-star pattern once more, patterns based on octagons and lozenges, a latchkey meander, and simple arrangements of squares and oblongs, decorated twenty or more rooms in two wings of an establishment whose many reminiscences of Mediterranean luxury villas have suggested that it was built either for the provincial governor or for a highly Romanised local potentate.

Geometric mosaics continued to be laid in the northern and western provinces during the second century, but the austere versions of the first century began to give way to more complex schemes, often with the addition of colour (principally red and yellow), or else reversing the traditional black on white to obtain white on black, that is a pattern 'in negative'. Italian models were now left behind, and the regions acquired greater artistic independence. The free-field black silhouette figure compositions which dominated the pavements of Rome and Ostia in the second and third centuries never acquired great currency in the North and West (one

43 Mosaic pavement at Ampurias (Spain): one of the early examples (first century AD) of the influence of the Italian black and white geometric style upon the mosaics of the western provinces. The scheme of eight-lozenge stars enclosing squares is one of the most popular and most characteristic of all patterns in Roman mosaics.

or two exceptions occur in the highly Romanised cities of southern Spain, such as Córdoba, Mérida and Itálica, all of which had a strong admixture of settlers of Italian stock). Instead, such figures as appeared were strictly subordinate to the geometric framework and were depicted in more or less realistic colours.

The typical pavements of the northern and western provinces from the second to the fourth century depend upon a more or less even structure of geometric ornament covering the surface. Divisions are effected, almost without exception, by various forms of guilloche, each strand of which is built up in graded colours changing across five lines of tesserae (characteristic sequences are black–red–orange–white–black, black–green–grey–white–black and black–olive–yellow–white–black) with a single-tessera white 'eye' at the point of overlap. The fields so created can be framed by further inner borders, either monochrome or polychrome, and they are usually filled with abstract ornaments or floral motifs of more or less complex form. The background is almost invariably a neutral white. Where figures (human or animal) or figure scenes occur, they are spread evenly through the scheme, each subject placed in a separate panel. Even if there is a principal scene at the centre, this never dominates the pavement in the way that the Greek-style *emblema* did, because the other figure panels are sufficiently important to draw attention away from it. Moreover, since the figures are shown on a neutral white ground which negates any effect of spatial recession, the old conflict between the pictorial form of polychrome figure scenes and the architectural function of the floor surface is largely avoided. The use of multiple figure panels also, of course, enabled the artist to avoid imposing a single viewpoint. Each subject could be oriented, as in the black-figure pavements of Italy, to favour the changing positions of a spectator moving round the room.

Within this general set of formulae there are numerous local variations reflecting the growth of independent groups of craftsmen creating their own distinctive style of product. The development of regional 'schools', and how they related to one another, are fascinating topics which have been much discussed in recent years. As yet, the available material is too limited and too imperfectly known for us to get a good overall picture of regional variations and patterns of influence across time. Doubtless, as more mosaics are discovered, and the publication of corpora (a process which is well advanced in some countries but not in others) brings ever more examples to notice, the situation will become gradually clearer – though whether it will ever be fully nuanced is an open question. For the moment we are much better informed about some regions, notably France, the Rhineland frontier and Britain, than about others.

One particular current of influence that has been discerned is from northern Italy to Provence and the Rhône valley, and from there to sites in western France, Switzerland and the Rhineland. This has been studied primarily from the perspective of the Rhône valley, where, during the late second and early third centuries, there emerged a flourishing school of mosaic workers, with major centres of production at Lyon (Lugdunum) and Vienne. The school's work features a number of distinctive schemes. Most characteristic are compositions based on square panels. In the simplest versions these are reminiscent of ceiling coffers and clearly derive from the imitation coffering of late Republican and early Imperial pavements in Italy; the individual panels are framed by different motifs, including herringbone, meander, superposed triangles, or squares laid point to point, and they are often separated by chains of smaller squares and rectangles containing lozenges (or sometimes a hexagon and two half-hexagons). This design was subsequently reproduced in mosaics at Saint-Prex and Orbe-Boscéaz (Vaud) in Switzerland. In the more elaborate versions, the panels are enlarged, and each is filled with a different pattern, often of repeating type (swastika latchkey meander, lozenge-stars and squares, perspective cubes, intersecting circles, four-point stars, or roundels containing various motifs). Evidently developed from prototypes in northern Italy, this scheme *à décor multiple* ('with multiple patterns') spread from the Rhône to other areas – north-west, for instance, to Ouzouër-sur-Trézée in the Loire region, and north-east to Besançon (Doubs) and to Münster-Sarmsheim in Rheinpfalz.

44   A rather different scheme evolved from North Italian models consists of a continuous swastika meander formed by a two-strand guilloche, often accompanied by black bands or by lines of superposed black triangles, and often arranged so as to leave panels at the corners and in the centre – panels which are decorated with floral motifs or figure subjects. Several examples are known in Lyon and Vienne; and from the Rhône valley the design travelled to Besançon and probably to Avenches (near Fribourg) in Switzerland, though the specimen from this last site replaces the black triangles with interlaced circles, producing a rather different effect.

Finally there are schemes of lozenge-stars. Patterns based on eight-lozenge stars were common throughout the Western Empire and their presence in the Rhône valley does not in itself denote any special genealogy; but a particular variant in which the pavement is enclosed by a frame of guilloche or the like which juts inwards between each lozenge-star is an idiosyncrasy which links southern Gaul with north-eastern Italy. The inward-jutting frame was subsequently used in combination with other schemes, including the 'multiple pattern' type. More unusually, a

44 *Detail of a pavement from Saint-Romain-en-Gal (Vienne, France), now in the British Museum. The scheme is based upon a meander pattern formed by a guilloche accompanied by chains of superposed black triangles; at each corner a square field is left available for a bust or pair of busts representing figures from the Dionysiac circle. Second half of the second century AD.*

number of pavements at Vienne and Lyon are based on six-lozenge stars alternating with hexagons; this scheme was again brought from northern Italy, where examples are known as early as the third quarter of the first century. From the Rhône it seems to have travelled to other parts of Gaul, appearing for example at Ouzouër-sur-Trézée and Périgueux.

These examples illustrate one broad chain of transmission of patterns and motifs within the mosaics of the north-west. The picture here presented is certainly generalised and masks a complicated pattern of movement and interplay between different groups of mosaicists in different centres. Recent research has added further nuances. For example, Autun (Augustodunum) in Burgundy has been recognised as a 'staging post' on the artistic route from the Rhône to the Rhineland and Mosel regions. There are close links, further, between Autun and Sens (Yonne), where a famous mosaic containing a representation of the sun-god reining in his horses was surrounded by a plant-scroll evidently carried out by the same circle of craftsmen as produced scrolls in mosaics at Autun and

45 *Detail of a geometric mosaic from Saint-Romain-en-Gal, now in Vienne, Musée Lapidaire. Schemes based upon hexagons and six-lozenge stars are among the specialities of the 'school' of mosaic-workers that emerged in the Rhône valley in the late second century AD. From here the design spread north and west to other sites in Gaul.*

Sennecey-le-Grand, near Tournus; in all cases the scroll was embellished
46 with a distinctive 'signature' in the form of little tendrils which bent at right angles, first left, then right, then left again, before tailing off. The same signature appears, in slightly more elaborate form, at Besançon. Such bizarre details indicate more clearly than the commoner motifs and schemes how individual mosaics were related to one another. In broader terms the Horses of the Sun mosaic shows its descent from the Rhône

46 *Detail of the Neptune mosaic at Autun (Augustodunum) in Burgundy (late second or early third century AD). The angular tendril growing from the vegetal scroll at the right is a distinctive feature which links this pavement with pavements at other sites in central and eastern France. All could be the work of the same circle of mosaicists.*

valley series by its use of a 'multiple pattern' scheme, with squares containing patterns of four-point stars, black and white triangles, black and white T shapes, and so forth.

The province for which workshop relationships have been most thoroughly explored is Britain, where intensive programmes of agricultural exploitation and building development have resulted in an unusual concentration of discoveries. Here the studies of David Smith are of paramount importance. In a first widespread surge of mosaic-laying, dated broadly to the second half of the second century and the early years of the third, and confined (as in Spain and the other northern provinces at this time) chiefly to the towns, Smith has identified two main groups of workshops. An eastern group, represented by examples from Verulamium, near St Albans (Hertfordshire), and Colchester (Essex), favoured schemes with a large central field flanked by subsidiary fields at the sides and smaller ones at the corners. One version has square and oblong fields with a great roundel 'underlying' the main framework; all fields are defined by the inevitable guilloche reinforced by additional borders with decorative motifs from the standard stock – wave-crest, sawtooth, superposed triangles, stylised plant-scrolls. Such panels as are reserved within the plethora of borders contain floral motifs or in one case a wine-bowl. Another version of the scheme presents a square central field and lunettes at the sides formed by the inward curvature of a great chain guilloche which frames the whole pavement. Here the central panel contains a figure subject, in one case a lion with a stag's head in its jaws, in another two chubby Cupids engaged in a wrestling match with a bird in attendance. The western group of workshops on the other hand, represented chiefly by pavements from Cirencester (Gloucestershire), Dorchester (Dorset) and Leicester, opted for schemes based on nine contiguous octagons. These were typically occupied by roundels containing abstract ornaments or floral motifs, though one example in Cirencester features mythological subjects (including the death of Actaeon and Silenus riding a donkey) and personifications of the four Seasons, and an example at Leicester has a peacock in the central position. As in the eastern group, these western mosaics incorporated a variety of framing motifs in which forms of guilloche were pre-eminent. All mosaics, both eastern and western, were polychrome, colours being based primarily on a palette of black, white, red and yellow, but with odd details (the eyes of the peacock's tail, for example) rendered in richer colours obtained from glass.

After a period of insecurity and economic stagnation, Britain saw a new wave of investment in mosaics in the late third and fourth centuries. This time, while some mosaics were still laid in towns, the bulk of the surviving material comes from the country villas to which the wealthy aristocracy of the province now diverted much of their capital. For this phase Smith and others have identified half a dozen groupings of workshops. In the south-west the so-called Durnovarian school, based in Dorchester, is characterised by a number of distinctive designs and motifs, including squat trees with wavy branches and lanceolate leaves, thin-stemmed plant-scrolls, tubby dolphins, and threshold panels with all-over patterns of back-to-back *peltae* (Amazons' shields); there was also a variety of animal and figure subjects, including many taken from mythology. One of the finest examples is the famous pavement from Hinton St Mary

47 (Dorset), now in the British Museum, which features a head of Christ and a representation of Bellerophon killing the Chimaera, plus scenes of dogs hunting deer and busts personifying the four Winds. Also in the south-west, Cirencester (ancient Corinium) is regarded as the centre of two groupings, the Corinian Orpheus school and the Corinian Saltire school, specialising respectively in a distinctive scheme of a lyre-playing Orpheus in a central tondo enclosed by concentric rings of animals and birds captivated by his music (the most spectacular example, at Woodchester in Gloucestershire, is the largest mosaic north of the Alps), and a distinctive

48 geometric composition based on large cross-shaped fields with a medallion at the centre and *pelta*-and-volute designs in the arms. Further afield, the other groupings include an East Midlands series of geometric pavements which Smith assigns to a Durobrivan school (after Durobrivae, or Water Newton in Cambridgeshire) and a Humberside and South Yorkshire group of figure mosaics with radial schemes, attributed to a Petuarian school (after Petuaria, near Brough on Humber).

Smith's groupings tend to oversimplify the situation, and he often makes them seem more homogeneous than they in fact were. Underlying them must have been a complex pattern of workshops and branch workshops, itinerant craftsmen and circulating pattern-books. Designs and motifs characteristic of one of the 'schools' are often found in the territory of another, and even in the same pavement as designs and motifs attributed to another 'school'. To take an unproblematic example, the Corinian Orpheus composition reappears in the repertoire of the Petuarian school, though the rings containing the birds and animals are now divided into separate panels by radial lines fanning out from the central Orpheus like the spokes of a wheel. Here, as Smith recognises, mosaicists active in the Humber region have imported an iconographic idea from the south-west but adapted it to a slightly different formulation. Elsewhere, however, the combination of one school's motifs with those of another has led Smith to argue that a pavement was laid in two phases, perhaps because of a repair

47 *Central roundel of a mosaic from Hinton St Mary (Dorset, Britain), now in the British Museum (fourth century AD). The bust, with the Christian monogram (chi-rho) behind its head and a pomegranate (symbolising eternal life) at each side, has been identified as a representation of Christ. The pavement shows many features (such as the almond-shaped leaves attached to the pomegranates) which are regarded as characteristic of the so-called Durnovarian School, based at nearby Dorchester.*

48 (right) *Remains of a mosaic pavement in a villa at Halstock (Dorset) in Britain. The mosaics from this site, excavated in the early 1970s, provide good examples of the work of David Smith's so-called Corinian Saltire school. Characteristic are the large cross-shaped elements with roundels at their mid-points and pairs of lozenges in the arms; filling motifs include* peltae *(Amazons' shields) with tightly scrolled tendrils springing from them.*

or a change of plan, by two separate teams from different parts of the province. It may, however, be simpler to argue for imitation or the exchange of ideas between workshops. By the same token, the division of 'Corinian' work into an Orpheus school and a Saltire school may be too hard and fast: it is difficult to believe that a team of mosaicists always specialised in figure work or in geometric work rather than choosing one or other type of pavement to suit a particular room or a particular client.

None of this invalidates the importance of Smith's analyses. It is clear that mosaics featuring certain schemes and motifs tend to be clustered in certain parts of the province and that these clusters reflect the activity of broad groupings of craftsmen based within the areas in question. Further research and new discoveries will no doubt refine our understanding of the interrelationships within and between the clusters.

Outside France and Britain the region in which local stylistic features have been most intensively studied is the Mosel valley and the Rhineland – a region focused on the two major centres of Trier and Cologne. The analysis is aided, as in Britain, by the large number of surviving mosaics. More than seventy-five were known in Trier in 1972, not counting those in the surrounding territory, and several more have been discovered since. These span the whole period from the first to the late fourth century, though with a special concentration in the late second and the first half of the third century, when the workshops of Trier forged a distinctive style which exercised influence over more than the immediate hinterland (there are even echoes in the pavements of the Durnovarian school in Britain). The favourite scheme in this style was centralised, with a dominant figure scene in a roundel or an octagon and further figure subjects in satellite panels at the sides and/or corners. Frames and subsidiary geometric elements were so numerous as to dominate the design, increasingly reducing the figure panels to isolated windows within an overwhelming mass of abstract ornament (as in the two most ambitious examples of the style, the
49 gladiator mosaic at Nennig and the Dionysiac mosaic in Cologne). Among the popular motifs, leaving aside the indispensable guilloche in its various forms, were the 'rainbow cable' which we encountered in the East, a similarly shaded band faceted by a zigzag line (used especially as a frame for lozenges), and meanders of simple type (battlement, right-angled Zs, and Zs with 'serifs' at the ends) again rendered in graded colours to suggest shading. A tightly spiralled wave-crest motif often framed the central roundel or octagon. Threshold panels or fill-in panels designed to adjust the square format of the main scheme to a rectangular room were decorated with all-over patterns based on *peltae* or with guilloche knots alternating with black and white squares and oblongs.

49 *Detail of the gladiator mosaic at Nennig (Mosel), an example of the polychrome compartmental mosaics produced in the Trier region during the late second and third centuries. This huge pavement from the central reception room in a grand villa featured scenes from the games of the amphitheatre (here a* venator *and a leopard) set within a complicated geometric framework decorated with various abstract motifs, notably different forms of guilloche.*

Figure subjects included not only perennial favourites such as Dionysus and his circle but also some slightly more unusual themes, such as the four-horse chariots and gladiatorial combats of contemporary popular entertainment. There was a particular penchant for what can be described as literary or intellectual subjects – not the abstract philosophical themes or literary episodes of Antioch but representations of the nine Muses, patronesses of the arts and learning, and of the famous personalities of literature and the arts. The so-called Monnus mosaic, found on the site of the Landesmuseum in Trier and named from the artist's signature, features nine large octagonal fields each containing a Muse and an exponent of her particular sphere of interest. All are identified by labels. The central field shows Calliope, the Muse of epic poetry, with Homer, the most venerated of all literary figures, and Ingenium, the personification of genius; the others that survive depict Euterpe instructing Hyagnis in the playing of the flutes, Urania explaining astronomy to Aratus, and Clio, the Muse of history, with Cadmus. Eight square fields in the interstices of the scheme contain a gallery of leading Greek and Latin authors: Hesiod, Menander, Ennius, Livy, Virgil, Cicero and two others. These subjects make a clear statement of the literary interests of the patron who commissioned the mosaic. Similar hymns to literary culture appear in other pavements. The

50

so-called Orator mosaic, sadly fragmentary, contained isolated figures in poses of declamation or with writing equipment (a bearded man may have been a professor of rhetoric, and four younger figures his students), as well as two seated females (Muses?) in attitudes suggesting disputation, and, in the central field, the deities Hermes (Mercury) and Athena (Minerva), patrons of the *gymnasium* (the ancient equivalent of a university) and its activities. A fragment from another mosaic preserves the seated figure of a greybeard holding a portable sundial; this has been identified as the philosopher and scientist Anaximander, who was said to have introduced the sundial to Greece. He perhaps formed part of a set of famous Greek writers and thinkers. From Cologne comes a pavement with the busts of seven such figures, each with his name inscribed in Greek: included were at least two of the Seven Sages (Chilon and Cleobulus) and at least two Athenian dramatists (Sophocles and Euripides), as well as the Cynic philosopher Diogenes, shown appropriately in the mouth of the storage jar which he made his home. All these mosaics represent a remarkable emphasis upon learning – one which testifies to the strength of classical education in this region in late Imperial times. Trier became an imperial capital under the Tetrarchs (at the end of the third century), and there is reason to believe that the court and its officials fostered a literary culture.

50 Detail of the Monnus mosaic at Trier. Named after the artist that signed it, this pavement is a good example of the interest in literary culture displayed by mosaics in the Rhineland and Mosel region. Here the Muse Euterpe teaches Hyagnis the art of playing the flutes; beyond, a bust of Menander. Rheinisches Landesmuseum, Trier.

51 Detail of a recently discovered mosaic pavement at Orbe-Boscéaz (Vaud) in Switzerland. Set in a classic 'multiple-pattern' scheme of the Rhône valley type, the roundel forms half of a unique two-part representation of the discovery of Achilles on Scyros. The trumpeter's clarion call rouses Achilles (shown in a separate panel) to throw off his female disguise and join the Greeks at Troy.

The literary flavour of these mosaics in Trier and Cologne is highly unusual. Elsewhere in the northern provinces the subject-matter of figure mosaics is overwhelmingly mythological. The Muses, admittedly, being mythical characters, occur elsewhere, for instance at Itálica and Arróniz in Spain; but the favourites of these provinces are, as in many other parts of the Empire, Dionysus and his circle, Venus (Aphrodite) and Cupid, and the 84 myths and fairy-tales beloved of Roman poets such as Ovid – the love- 85 affairs of Jupiter (Zeus), for example, Theseus and the Minotaur, Bellerophon killing the Chimaera, Hylas seized by the water-nymphs, Orpheus and the animals, the labours of Heracles, the musical contest of Apollo and Marsyas, and many others. The heroic themes of Homeric epic are surprisingly rare, though the romantic tale of Achilles' sojourn, disguised as a girl, at the court of King Lycomedes of Scyros appears on two late (fourth- and fifth-century) mosaics in Spain, as well as at Saint-Romain-en-Gal (a suburb of Vienne) in France, at Orbe-Boscéaz in 51

52 (left) *Cosmological mosaic at Mérida (Spain). This astonishing composition containing upwards of forty figures represented the civilised world by means of personifications, celestial in the upper half and terrestrial in the lower. The multi-figure format, the use of labels and the central role of Alexandria all suggest an East Mediterranean source, even though the labels are in Latin rather than Greek.*

53 (below) *Detail of the cosmological mosaic at Mérida (fig. 52), showing Nubs (Cloud) being carried along by Notus (the South Wind), with the heads of the chariot-horses of Oriens (the Rising Sun) below. Late second or third century AD.*

Switzerland, and possibly also at Keynsham (Somerset) in Britain. The themes of Roman legend are even rarer. A famous mosaic from Low Ham in Britain illustrates successive episodes from the story of Dido and Aeneas, recalling the account in the fourth book of Virgil's *Aeneid*. A panel in a mosaic at Frampton, also in Britain, showed Aeneas breaking off the golden bough which was his passport to the Underworld. The wolf and twins of Rome's foundation legend are depicted at Aldborough in Britain and a couple of sites in Spain. Otherwise there is nothing Roman. As in other forms of privately sponsored art in the Roman world, the stories illustrated were chosen almost exclusively from the stock of ancient Greece.

Almost as rare as the legends of Rome are personifications. Though the calendar months appear on the Monnus mosaic at Trier, and the four Winds and the four Seasons – especially the Seasons – occur with relative frequency, there seems to have been little interest in the representations of virtues and other abstract ideas that had gained currency in Antioch and the East. The bust of a female holding a cornucopia (horn of plenty) which is found in a few mosaics in Britain and Spain, and which must be identified as Abundance or the like, is a special case in that Abundance came nearer to having the status of a goddess than most abstract concepts.

The one major exception to the rule is the astonishing 'cosmological mosaic' at Mérida, which presented a grand allegory of the civilised world. 52-3 Constructed in banks of figures distributed over the whole of an arched field 4.68 metres high and 3.68 metres wide, this composition included between forty and fifty personifications, ranging from cosmic concepts such as Heaven and Time at the top down through the lower atmosphere (the rising and setting sun, clouds, winds, mountains and snow) to terrestrial and geographical ideas (Nature, the Seasons, the Euphrates, the Nile) and personifications of the sea and seaborne trade (Ocean, Calm, Navigation, Abundance) at the bottom – all focused on a largely missing central figure which may have symbolised Eternity. Beneath this last, on the axis of the picture, are Portus and Pharus, clearly (from the position of Portus next to the Nile) representations of the port and lighthouse of Alexandria. This mosaic is unique among the pavements of the West, and, given the illusionistic Classical style, the central role of Alexandria, and the reliance upon labels (albeit here Latin rather than Greek) to identify the figures, it can only have been the work of an artist from the East.

A relatively limited number of mosaics depicted scenes from life. Such are the references to popular entertainments already mentioned. The charioteers of the circus appear not just at Trier but also in Portugal (at Conimbriga), in Spain (at Mérida, Itálica, Córdoba, and Jerez de los Caballeros, south of Badajos), in Gaul (at Sainte-Colombe, another suburb of Vienne), in southern Germany (at Rottweil), and in Britain (at Rudston

92 in North Humberside). The games of the amphitheatre, including beast-
hunts and gladiatorial combats, are illustrated not just in the mosaics of the

49 Trier region (at Nennig and Bad Kreuznach); they occur also at Augst

8 (Basel) and Vallon (Vaud) in Switzerland and again at Rudston in Britain.
More striking are those mosaics which show chariot-races in a complete
circus, represented from above in a kind of bird's-eye perspective. Examples
occur at Itálica, Barcelona and Gerona in Spain and at Horkstow (South
Humberside) in Britain. Finally, there are scenes of hunting in the wild –

93 notably on a fine mosaic from Lillebonne in northern France, where four
friezes enclosing a central roundel with a mythological subject (a god seiz-
ing a nymph) represent the different phases of an expedition: firstly the
sacrifice to Diana, goddess of the hunt, then the departure of the huntsmen,
one leading a decoy stag, then the actual chase, with horsemen and hounds
in full career, and finally the prelude to the kill, in which a huntsman aims
an arrow at a wild stag that has been lured from cover by the decoy.

The circus and hunting mosaics belong to the fourth century, and their
relatively ambitious, multi-figure format is alien to the general tradition of
the northern provinces. It is highly probable that they reflect a current of
influence from North Africa, where this type of composition and a taste
for subjects from daily life had become established at an earlier date. To
trace the emergence of this more worldly repertoire it is to Africa that we
must now turn.

6 ROMAN AFRICA

In Roman Africa, that is the Latin-speaking provinces of Africa Proconsularis (corresponding roughly to modern Tunisia and Tripolitania), Numidia (the eastern part of Algeria) and Mauretania (Morocco and the western part of Algeria), mosaic arrived late. Despite the existence of a Punic tradition of decorated mortar pavements which stretched back to the fourth century BC (Chapter 3), the first known examples of complete tessellated pavements are no earlier than the late first century AD. This delay in accepting what was by now one of the hallmarks of Mediterranean civilisation was doubtless due to the initial slowness of the general process of Romanisation in these regions. When mosaic did appear, it was initially, like early work in Spain and Gaul, under strong Italian influence. The first examples are at Utica, the original capital of the province of Africa and a highly Romanised city, which has yielded black and white geometric pavements whose patterns are closely related to examples in Italy.

The illusionistic pictures of eastern mosaic gained no firm footing in Africa. The mosaics from the Villa of Dar Buc Amméra at Zliten in Tripolitania, which include fine pictorial panels of Hellenistic type (a series of rural scenes, with peasants at work in the fields and threshing corn), seem to represent an isolated case of eastern influence at a later, perhaps early third-century, date. Generally speaking, the geometric frameworks and non-spatial figure scenes of the West prevailed. The major difference is that African mosaicists quickly rejected the black and white style of Italy in favour of polychromy. The reasons for this choice are unclear, but one factor may have been the geological resources of northern and eastern Tunisia, where the African tradition first developed. The availability of coloured stone such as the richly variegated red, pink and yellow marble (*giallo antico*) from the quarries of Chemtou may have inspired artists to experiment with a coloristic treatment which then became widely fashionable.

The practice of laying such mosaics became well established during the second century. Among the earliest examples are the pavements of two sets

54 of baths at Acholla. Here the black and white style has been joined by a polychrome technique (though still on a white ground), and the compositions already show an independent spirit. The great pavement from the *frigidarium* (cold room) of the so-called Baths of Trajan is notable for its use of decorative half-animal, half-plant forms – the 'grotesques' which are a feature of the wall and ceiling paintings of the last years of Pompeii and generally of the paintings of Rome itself in the second half of the first century. Rendered predominantly in golden yellow tones, with orange and grey-green playing subsidiary roles, the ornament recalls the gilded reliefs of the emperor Nero's fabulous Golden House. The Acholla mosaic was clearly designed by an artist familiar with this Italian style. There is no known Italian precedent, however, for its transference to a floor. The scheme, indeed, with its diagonal ribs decorated with elaborate candelabrum ornaments, looks like an attempt to imitate the effect of a vault decoration – not one of the simple coffer schemes found in Italian pavements but a scheme designed for one of the groined cross-vaults which were becoming increasingly important in the monumental architecture of the period.

From the more intensively Romanised regions of Africa Proconsularis mosaics spread westwards into Numidia and Mauretania. Some of the remoter western sites did not latch on to the fashion till relatively late, but wherever it gained a foothold the art of mosaic enjoyed spectacular success. In Proconsularis, at least, its golden age began in the second half of the second century when the province experienced a period of prosperity, attested by major public building projects and by the rise of Africans to important positions at Rome, culminating in the accession of an African emperor, Septimius Severus, in 193. During the third century, while the

European provinces suffered from barbarian incursions and political in-stability, Africa remained relatively peaceful and benefited from its oil and grain production to maintain a healthy economy; there was thus continued investment in housing at a time when little was happening on the Empire's northern frontiers. The level of Africa's prosperity must have increased with the recovery of the Empire in the fourth century, when Carthage is reported to have been the world's third city after Rome and Constantinople. Only in the fifth century did decay set in.

Perhaps surprisingly, the bulk of Africa's mosaics come from the towns. There is as yet little evidence of the rich villa culture which developed in the fourth century in provinces such as Spain, Gaul and Britain. This situation may simply be the result of the lack of archaeological investigation of rural sites, because the mosaics themselves testify to the importance of country estates to the municipal elite. At the moment, however, almost all of the material that we have to study is derived from urban contexts.

The extent to which town houses were furnished with mosaics is astonishing. The proportion of houses that had mosaics is far greater than in other parts of the Roman world. So too is the number of rooms within a house that were decorated in this way. In many houses that have been excavated, for example the House of Neptune at Acholla, the House of the Laberii at Oudna (ancient Uthina) and the House of the Nymphs at Nabeul (Neapolis), and indeed in whole quarters of towns such as Pupput, Utica, Bulla Regia and El Djem (ancient Thysdrus), virtually every room apart from service rooms was paved with a geometric or figured mosaic. Moreover, it was not just houses that were so paved, but also public baths, and indeed some other public buildings (though the more important received pavements of *opus sectile*). All this confirms the social desirability of mosaic paving in African cities: it was a *sine qua non* of the urban life-style. The content of the decorations can therefore be expected to tell us much about the tastes and preoccupations of town-dwellers in this part of the Roman world.

Africa is noted principally for its polychrome figure mosaics, with scenes distributed freely over the floor surface, as in the black-figure compositions of Italy. But there were many more mosaics which employed geometric schemes, with or without figure compartments in the style of the northern provinces. It can rarely be claimed, however, that these geometric or compartmentalised pavements lack interest or are mere replicas of specimens north of the Mediterranean. Many of them show a degree of inventiveness that is rare in other parts of the Empire.

Among the types of geometric composition which became especially associated with Africa was the 'floral style'. This derived from the floral style found in Italy, for example in Hadrian's Villa at Tivoli, but from the first it was carried out in a range of colours, not just black on white. In all instances the structure of the scheme was geometric, but most of the lines were interpreted in vegetal terms. The standard compositions were based on contiguous or intersecting circles formed by vine or ivy tendrils or by other kinds of foliate stems. Further complexity was introduced by the inclusion of square compartments in alternation with the circles, and in such cases the corners of the squares were sometimes linked by spindle-shaped elements. These patterns tended to become heavier, with acanthus fronds replacing the more delicate vine tendrils, and with thick laurel wreaths sometimes enclosing the roundels; at the same time the subsidiary ornament proliferated to the point that the white of the background was increasingly submerged. Such designs could be used in isolation, or they could serve as a framework within which were set figural elements: in some cases simply birds, animals, busts and masks; in others human forms, such as the charioteer Scorpianus in a mosaic at Carthage, or the Muses in another mosaic from the Carthage area, now in the British Museum.

A particularly fine range of floral mosaics was created by a school of
55 mosaicists based at Timgad (ancient Thamugadi) in Numidia. Here the richness and variety of the compositions, which included not just linear

55 Detail of a floral mosaic at Timgad (Algeria). This sumptuous pattern, which spread over the whole pavement of the principal reception room in the House of the Pool, provides an excellent example of the distinctive floral style of Timgad, in which shapes outlined by split acanthus fronds are filled in with various colours, especially black and red. This contrasts with the normal treatment of African floral mosaics, in which the patterns are merely in outline on a white background. Third century AD. Timgad Museum.

56 *Detail of mosaic with arching 'cables' and plant-sprigs framing peacock feathers, from the House of the Dionysiac Procession at El Djem (Thysdrus) in Tunisia (second half of the second century AD). This design, or variants upon it, including versions in which the cables grow from craters (wine-bowls) and the peacocks' feathers are replaced by plants or flowers, was especially popular in Africa. El Djem Museum.*

tendrils but bell- and heart-shaped arrangements of acanthus leaves with red and black infills, turned these ancient stone floor-coverings into the visual counterparts of the woven carpets now sold in the modern cities of North Africa.

The ways in which geometric patterns could be enlivened by vegetal elements were legion. A popular motif found in the region of Sousse (ancient Hadrumetum) and El Djem was a scale-like pattern of arching 'cables' placed one above the other; these cables sometimes sprang from *craters* (wine-bowls) or leaf calyces, sometimes merely rested on the arch below, but in every case the semicircular spaces contained a flower, a leafy plant or (more commonly) a peacock's feather. In another scheme a network 56 of sinuous tendrils was overlaid on a pattern of intersecting cable circles, so as to appear to weave in and out of it.

A popular theme which was purely geometric was the so-called 'cushion' pattern – a composition of elliptical shapes alternating with concave-sided quadrilaterals (the 'cushions' of the name). These fields contained more or less complex floral motifs or occasionally figural elements, and their frames consisted of thick black lines accompanied by inner borders of 'cables', wave-crest, shaded battlement meander, or lines with dentils attached. Like the floral style, this pattern was capable of indefinite expansion and was ideally suited to rooms of passage, such as corridors or the ambulatories of peristyles.

In addition to systems of decoration which were geometrically constructed, other African specialities were imitation marbling and free-

growing vegetation. Imitation marbling, a fashion found especially in
Proconsularis, is a curious concept,
in that it uses one type of cut-stone
technique, namely tessellation, to
imitate another, namely *opus sectile*.
The tesserae are arranged to suggest
the veins of coloured marbles,
breccias and alabasters, and the
intention was patently to simulate
pavements in these more expensive
materials. One might have expected

the costs involved in the more time-consuming practice of piecing
together small tesserae to have outweighed the costs of purchasing the
actual exotic stones in question, but presumably problems of availability
and supply, and perhaps the relative wage levels of the craftsmen, dictated
otherwise. It is significant that this imitative technique was often used in
baths (for instance in the *frigidarium* of the south-east baths at Maktar), a
type of building in which the ideal, albeit rarely attained, was clearly real
sectile. Whatever the economic considerations, the colourful abstract patterns which resulted from the mosaicist's attempt to reproduce the various
types of marble created a striking mode of decoration in their own right.

Free-growing vegetal decorations are those in which vines or the like
emerge from leaf calyces or *craters* at the corners of a pavement and spread
in sinuous curves towards the centre. The sprawling vegetation so created
is peopled with birds and Cupids and, in conformance with the idea of
fertility and fruitfulness that the design evokes, there may be busts or full-
length figures personifying the four Seasons, one towards each angle, and
a representation of the fertility god Dionysus, or of figures and legends
connected with him, at the centre. In an example from Haïdra (Tunisia)
the branches growing from each corner were endowed with the flowers
and fruits of a different season: olives for Winter, roses for Spring, corn for
Summer, and grapes for Autumn. Appropriate species of birds accompanied
them. All-over vegetation of this type had appeared in second-century
mosaics in Italy, but once again the Italian antecedents were exclusively
drawn in black on a white ground, whereas the African examples were
fully polychrome. The Italian examples were also simpler and more
schematised than the luxuriant growth of the plant forms in Africa.

Another variant upon the vegetal theme was a type of decoration in
which loose branches, fruit, flowers and garlands were strewn in studied
disorder. The idea for this design may go back ultimately to the 'unswept

57 (above) *Panel of
imitation marble in
Carthage: representative
of a peculiarly African
fashion of using mosaic to
reproduce the coloured
lakes and veins of exotic
stones used in* opus
sectile *and wall veneer.
This particular panel,
which is in grey, green,
yellow, white and black,
may be designed to
reproduce Carystian
marble (cipollino) from
Euboea in Greece.*

58 *Vine mosaic from El
Djem. Pavements with
vines or other plants
growing from each corner
are a popular theme in
Africa: the branches are
often, as here, populated
with birds and Cupids
gathering grapes, while
Dionysiac figures,
including satyrs with
wild animals, are depicted
at the margins. The
central field contains a
scene of children sporting
with Dionysus' elderly
follower Silenus. Second
half of third century* AD.
El Djem Museum.

dining-room' of Hellenistic times, but a more immediate precedent is provided by two Nilotic mosaics from El Alia, near El Djem, where the flora, fauna and human activities of the Nile in its flood season are illustrated in the same scatter-gun technique on a neutral white ground (in contrast with the coherent landscape setting of the Nile mosaic at Palestrina). Whatever its sources, the strewn foliage style was effectively exploited in a number of third- and fourth-century mosaics, notably the pavement which gives its name to the House of the Aviary at Carthage. Here the surface of a courtyard surrounding an octagonal garden was decorated with a large variety of birds and animals distributed among the standard plant sprigs so as to achieve an even network of motifs which could be appreciated from many different angles. The same strewn foliage appears in the border of the famous Mosaic of the Horses, also at Carthage, this time as a background for figures of children hunting birds and small animals.

All these different types of geometric, floral and vegetal decoration demonstrate the vitality and invention of the African mosaicists. But it is for their figure work that they are deservedly celebrated.

The range of figure subjects chosen includes many from the standard stock. The nine Muses and the four Seasons, each carefully distinguished by appropriate attributes, were as popular in Africa as in the northern provinces. The months are depicted, together with the Seasons, in mosaics from Carthage and El Djem, respectively in the form of female personifications and of scenes representing activities peculiar to each month. A striking pavement from Bir-Chana in Tunisia contains the seven busts of the planetary deities symbolising the days of the week, with their animals and the signs of the zodiac (all in panels set in surrounds of imitation breccia). Marine aquaria, with fish and fishermen distributed in a watery medium indicated by zigzag lines, were frequently chosen for the pavements of baths; the composition was sometimes dominated by a huge face of the sea-god Oceanus, crabs' claws growing from his head and seaweed from his moustaches. Of strictly mythological themes the most common, as in the northern provinces, are those associated with Dionysus and Venus, though the two particular favourites - the triumphal scenes of Dionysus riding his tiger-drawn chariot and Venus sitting in a giant shell carried by Tritons or sea-centaurs – are not much found outside Africa. The triumph of Neptune, shown standing, with or without his consort Amphitrite, in a chariot drawn by sea-horses, is also popular. Otherwise the repertoire is broadly similar to that of the northern provinces except that some northern favourites, such as Bellerophon and the Chimaera, are not attested, while some subjects which do appear are virtually unparalleled elsewhere in the Empire: for example, Dionysus' adventure with the Tyrrhenian

59

pirates in a pavement from a house at Dougga (ancient Thugga) in Tunisia, the forge of the Cyclops also from Dougga, and the marriage of Peleus and Thetis at Cherchel (Iol Caesarea) and Choba (Ziama-Mansouriah) in Algeria. In the House of the Nymphs at Nabeul a series of figure scenes includes subjects apparently not otherwise attested in Roman art, some of which have still not been satisfactorily explained.

Many of these figure subjects are shown in conventional manner within panels and friezes, though usually upon a neutral white ground. But a few of the compositions use novel methods akin to those of the black-figure pavements of Italy. In the pavement of Peleus and Thetis at Cherchel, for example, two successive episodes, one showing the presentation of Thetis to Peleus and the other their marriage, are represented within one large undivided field but opposite ways up, each oriented to be seen from different sides of the room. In other cases, when successive episodes are combined, they are normally set the same way up but conventionally one above the other in separate registers. This is the mode employed in a pavement from Tipasa (in Algeria) representing scenes from the life of Achilles: his introduction to the centaur Chiron who was to be his tutor is shown at the top and his discovery on Scyros below. There is no indication of

60 *Achilles mosaic from Tipasa (Algeria) in Algiers Museum. Illustrated are two episodes from Achilles' early life: his mother Thetis handing him over to the centaur Chiron to be educated, and his discovery disguised as a girl at the court of King Lycomedes of Scyros (cf. fig. 51). The representation of the action in superposed registers on a neutral white ground conforms to a favourite scheme in African pavements.*

setting, not even a ground-line (though, oddly, hints of cast shadows appear). The figures form conventional rows distributed across a neutral white field.

This way of arranging figures at different levels within an undivided field seems to have emerged during the late second century, and to have been the result primarily of the mosaicists' response to a new range of subjects which African clients now began to demand – subjects concerned with the everyday activities and preoccupations of the clients themselves. These were the popular entertainments of the amphitheatre and the circus, the hunting which was a favourite pastime of the local aristocracy, and generally the maintenance of the stud-farms and agricultural estates which were the source of their wealth.

Representations connected with the amphitheatre fall into three main groups: those that illustrate the actual events of a show or shows that took place there, those that commemorate a show by cataloguing the animals that were exhibited in it, and those that refer to the games indirectly by

61 *Amphitheatre mosaic from Smirat, now in Sousse Museum.* The venatores *and leopards taking part in the combats are all labelled with their names, and the long inscription in the middle, accompanying a figure of a youth carrying four bags of money, records the munificence of one Magerius in paying the cost of the show: the pavement evidently recorded a specific occasion. Magerius himself and the deities Diana and Dionysus are also represented. Midsecond century* AD.

means of the emblems of the different 'clubs' of *venatores* (hunters), the toreadors of the ancient arena. To the first category belongs a second-century mosaic from a house in El Djem, one of the earliest examples of a free composition occupying the greater part of its pavement. Like most of the mosaics which represent the events of the amphitheatre it is arranged in a series of isolated incidents which face outwards, so as to be appreciated by a viewer walking round the periphery of the room. At the centre is a platform with trophies standing on the corners; along the sides wild beasts (bears and leopards) prowl; and at the corners, illustrating a common practice of the Roman arena, condemned criminals or prisoners of war are served up, bound head and foot, as fodder for the leopards. All the action takes place on a plain white ground, with no indication of space other than a few vaguely suggested ground-lines and shadows. Similar in composition and in its treatment of space is a mosaic from Smirat, not far from El Djem, which shows duels between *venatores* and leopards. Here, however, there are additional figures, and information on the circumstances of the display is provided by inscriptions. All the *venatores* and animals are named, as is a prominent standing figure, Magerius, who, as a lengthy inscription in the middle of the pavement reveals, paid generous

61

sums of money to recompense the performers for the leopards that were killed. The role of the pavement was, in fact, primarily commemorative. The house from which it comes apparently belonged to Magerius, who commissioned the work to remind himself, his visitors and posterity of an act of conspicuous civic munificence. The splendour of his munificence is enhanced by the presence of the deities Dionysus and Diana, patrons of the amphitheatre, who oversee proceedings and tacitly give the benefactor their blessing.

Of the second category of amphitheatre-related mosaic the most notable examples are from Carthage, from Radès (the ancient Makula, a small town near Carthage), and from the House of the Ostriches at Sousse. In each case animals are distributed at different levels within a plain white field, and in each case there are hints that a specific show, no doubt sponsored by the client who commissioned the mosaic, was commemorated. In the Carthage mosaic numbers were written against the animals, apparently to record the number of the relevant species exhibited; at Radès, while a bull has a number against it, the wilder animals (boars and bears) are individually named – clear evidence that the mosaic alludes to a particular

62

62 Animal catalogue from the House of the Ostriches at Sousse. The animals, which occupy of a T-shaped area in a triclinium (three-couch dining-room), with venatores *at the foot of the T, refer to amphitheatre shows mounted by the house-owner. Further such figures, including a named* venator, *appear elsewhere in the house. Mid-third century AD.*

event. In the Sousse mosaic there are no names or numbers, but the head of the T-shaped field containing the animals is occupied by four *venatores* whose differing dress and equipment are recorded in such minute detail that there can again be little doubt that a specific show was intended. Elsewhere in the same house there was a panel commemorating the killing of two bears by a *venator* named Neoterius.

The third category of amphitheatre mosaic, that in which references are made to the teams of *venatores* and their emblems, is a more amorphous and problematic grouping. Many of the references, which depend on a knowledge of contemporary practices undocumented in surviving literature, are difficult for us to understand. Important clues to their elucidation have been obtained from a mosaic panel at El Djem, the so-called Mosaic of the Bulls and the Banquet, which depicts five banqueters enjoying themselves (as their comments, written above their heads, confirm) round a semi-circular table while two attendants exhort them not to disturb the bulls, which are shown sleeping in the foreground. The five banqueters all have different attributes, which, with the aid of representations in other mosaics, have been identified as the emblems of five different clubs or teams: an ivy leaf; a crown with three spikes, one of which bears the letter S; a crown with five radiating spikes, one of which carries a fish; a stalk of a plant identified as millet, and a bull-goad in the form of a crescent on a stick. It seems that members of the rival teams are drinking together on the eve of a show, and that the bulls below are the animals against which they are to be pitted on the next day. Elsewhere the emblems of the clubs are linked with numbers, which evidently had symbolic (or conventional) meaning. Inscriptions such as that of the Magerius mosaic enable us to learn some of the clubs' names. The crescent on a stick, for example, was the emblem of the Telegenii, whose number was three; and the fish was the emblem of the Pentasii, whose number was five. The emblems and their associated numbers appear in mosaic pavements in many houses, sometimes in panels illustrating fights between wild animals, which had presumably been mounted by the clubs in question, sometimes simply as a threshold panel or within the general decorative ensemble. In such cases we can imagine that the householder was proclaiming his allegiance to a particular club, much like the supporters of modern football teams.

The second popular entertainment celebrated in mosaics was the chariot-racing of the circus. The four factions that took part in the races, the Reds, the Blues, the Whites and the Greens, excited as much (if not more) passionate support and rivalry as the teams of *venatores* in the amphitheatre; it is not therefore surprising to find mosaics that celebrated the success of a particular charioteer and his team of horses. In such cases

names are generally supplied, and the charioteer and horses are set in self-contained compartments within a larger pavement decorated with a geometric or floral design. Scorpianus at Carthage, already mentioned, is a case in point, shown with his chariot team in profile in a floral-style pavement. At Dougga the charioteer Eros, a favourite of the green faction, stands in frontal view wielding his whip over a team of horses of which the inner pair is named as Amandus and Frunitus. Particularly interesting is the Mosaic of the Horses at Carthage, a huge pavement divided into square panels decorated alternately in *opus sectile* and in mosaic; the mosaic panels carried isolated figures of charioteers from each faction, of the attendants and officials of the circus, and of favourite horses. Neither horses nor charioteers are here named, but the horses are accompanied by small-scale images, taken from mythology or from the everyday world, which apparently served as pictograms for their names: it seems that the owner of the dining-room in which the pavement was laid had designed them as the basis of a kind of party game to entertain his guests.

In these mosaics, as stated, the charioteers and horses appear in independent compartments, whether as a team or (as in the Mosaic of the Horses) separately. More novel is the type of mosaic which shows the whole circus with a race taking place within it. Only five more or less complete examples survive – two in Carthage, one in Silin in Tripolitania, one in Volubilis in Morocco, and one of Byzantine date at Gafsa (ancient Capsa) in southern Tunisia – and two of them are parodies which substitute birds (geese, parrots and peacocks are preserved) for the chariot-horses; but

there is little doubt that they represent a well-established form of circus illustration evolved in Africa which inspired later imitations in other provinces, notably Spain. Unlike the mosaics that depicted events in the amphitheatre, this type showed not only the action but also the building that contained it. There were inevitably some inconsistencies of perspective, as illustrated by the earliest version, one of those from Carthage. While the interior of the circus is laid out in bird's-eye view, the external façade at the bottom, the central *spina* round which the chariots turned and the far side of the auditorium, with two buildings surmounting it, are all shown in normal horizontal perspective. So too are the chariots involved in the race, two of them above the *spina* and two below. The starting gates at the right end of the track are again depicted in horizontal perspective but at right angles to the other elements. In other words, visual appearances have been sacrificed in favour of clarity of presentation. As in many other 'documentary' mosaics in North Africa, the result is a largely schematised rendering that spreads the action over the available surface without imposing spatial illusion or too forcefully prioritising a single viewpoint.

Scenes of hunting and of rural life may be more briefly summarised. All involve figures and animals in outdoor settings, and all adopt the new type of composition in which episodes are ranged freely over the whole pavement. The background is always white, and landscape elements, like the figures, are set at different levels with isolated ground-lines; there is thus no unified space such as might cause an unsettling visual penetration of the surface. At the same time, the presence of landscape (trees, bushes, distant hills, buildings) tends to impose a single orientation. A typical arrangement is in two or three registers with a continuous terrain at the bottom and a line of hills, trees or buildings rounding off the composition at the top.

The subject-matter is essentially realistic, even where some iconographic types are borrowed from the traditional repertoire. A good example of the hunting series is an apsidal mosaic of a boar-hunt from Carthage in which huntsmen and dogs confront the boar in the lowest register, drive it into a netted enclosure in the middle, and carry home its carcass suspended

64 Circus mosaic from Carthage, now in the Bardo Museum, Tunis. The interior of the circus is shown in bird's-eye view, while the four chariot teams appear in normal horizontal perspective, two above and two below the central spina *round which they raced. Early third century* AD.

65 *Apsidal mosaic from Carthage depicting a boar-hunt, now in the Bardo Museum, Tunis. The action reads from the bottom to the top, with the dead boar being carried home in the uppermost register. First half of third century* AD.

from a pole at the top. These are the events of a real boar-hunt described in narrative sequence. A mosaic of a hare-hunt from El Djem is similarly true to life but recounts the details from top to bottom, the huntsmen setting out in the upper register, discovering the hare hiding in a brake in the middle register, and giving chase to it at the bottom.

In the late third and fourth centuries there was an increasing taste for exotic hunts, in which the prey was not everyday game such as boars, hares or deer, but tropical creatures of the kind that were displayed in the amphitheatre. The hunts are still represented by means of multi-level compositions, and the details continue to ring true: a baited box is used to trap a lioness in a mosaic from the Dermech area of Carthage, and various wild beasts are corralled within netting in a scene from the House of Isguntus at Hippo Regius (Bône in Algeria). But these scenes cannot now represent the normal activities of local aristocrats; they have become subsumed within a grander theme – the big-game hunts organised for the collection of beasts for the amphitheatre.

Where hunt scenes remain rooted in the real life of African landowners they are shown in a setting which clearly indicates that the action takes place on or near a country estate. This is achieved most characteristically by including a representation, in a prominent position, of a farm or villa. The same buildings appear also on mosaics which illustrate the life of the estate in general terms. An example from the House of the Laberii at Oudna includes a boar-hunt and a unique scene of a man disguised in a goat-skin stalking partridges, but also contains standard rural activities: a shepherd with his flock, a ploughman driving a team of oxen, a man drawing water from a well. Here most of the scenes are as usual distributed at different levels on independent ground-lines, but some of them are at right angles to the rest, along the sides of the pavement, so that the spectator is offered three different viewpoints.

While some of the rural mosaics are doubtless simply idyllic fancies designed to evoke an image of country life for town-dwellers, there are others that clearly record the activities of a specific estate, such as the mosaic of Dominus Julius from Carthage, which shows a manor-house at the centre, with the lord and lady receiving gifts of farm produce above and below. The style of the building, with its high substructure and corner towers, apparently reflects the reality of villa architecture in the fourth century. A similar building is one of three depicted in the semicircular mosaics from a three-apsed room in a house at Tabarka (ancient Thabraca) in Tunisia. Like the Dominus Julius mosaic, these may record specific details of the country estate of the mosaicist's client. Other mosaics depict stud-farms. In an example from the House of Sorothus at Sousse we see mares and foals grazing against a rocky landscape, while at each corner

66 *Dominus Julius mosaic from Carthage, now in the Bardo Museum, Tunis. Late fourth century AD. At the centre is a fortified villa; above and below, the lord and lady of the estate appear in scenes symbolising the activities and production of each of the four seasons. Such documentary scenes of rural life are typical of African pavements.*

there is a medallion containing a pair of named horses confronted across a palm-tree; the horses are branded with the name of Sorothus, who is thus identified as their owner. There can be little doubt that the mosaic was commissioned to celebrate Sorothus' stables, which presumably reared horses for the chariot-races of the circus. It was a similar sense of pride that, many centuries later, was to lead British aristocrats to hang paintings of successful race-horses in their stately homes.

Rather different from these statements of landed wealth is a remarkable
67 series of illustrations of agricultural labours from Cherchel. These are arranged in superposed registers, but with rather heavier ground surfaces and more prominent landscape elements than the examples already considered: the ground and the vegetation here play an integral part in the operations represented – tilling the soil, sowing the seed, hoeing the vineyard, and pruning the vines. What is most noteworthy, however, is that the operations, which are represented in graphic detail, are being performed by peasant labourers. There is no place for the lord of the manor, and no hint of aristocratic activities such as hunting and horse-breeding. A fragment of another pavement from Cherchel, which provides an equally graphic illustration of grape-treading, indicates that such 'grass-roots' realism was a special interest of patrons and mosaicists in this region.

67 *Agricultural scenes on a third-century mosaic at Cherchel (Algeria). The scenes illustrated show ploughing and sowing; below (not visible) comes the tending of the vineyards in winter. The importance of the landscape setting, the degree of realism, and the focusing upon peasant labour rather than aristocratic pastimes are all unusual among African mosaics depicting rural life.*

The general African predilection for subjects taken from the real world rather than from mythology, and the form of representation which distributes scenes rendered in full colour over a broad undifferentiated white surface, are distinctive features that have given rise to the term 'African style'. This African style ultimately spread beyond the shores of Africa and came to exercise some influence in other parts of the Empire.

The area where this influence was most directly felt was, not surprisingly, the nearby island of Sicily. Here a number of mosaics laid in the fourth century show such close similarities to pavements in Africa, and especially in Africa Proconsularis, that it seems almost certain that they were the work of African mosaicists brought over to carry out special commissions. The most striking example of African work in Sicily is the fabulous villa at Piazza Armerina, probably to be dated to the third quarter of the century, where there were more than 3,500 square metres of mosaics, all polychrome and mostly figured. Pavement after pavement, whether mythological or 'documentary', can be paralleled in Africa. A mosaic of children hunting small animals among scattered plants, for example, repeats the motif of the border of the Mosaic of the Horses at Carthage. A mosaic of vintaging Cupids has several African counterparts. A grand circus mosaic, laid out like the circus mosaic in Carthage, occupies a whole room in the baths – a room appropriately shaped like a circus. There is also a circus of bird-drawn chariots like the African examples from Carthage and Volubilis. The pavements in the ambulatories of the great peristyle reproduce a favourite African design of laurel wreaths containing animal heads. Only one pavement, that of a great trilobate hall in the southern part of the villa, cannot be easily paralleled in Africa: it shows the labours of Heracles, rendered on a much larger scale than the other figure scenes in the villa and in a style of baroque overstatement, with violent poses and bold foreshortening, that puts it in a class of its own.

The best examples of pavements with an African connection are the two hunt mosaics of Piazza Armerina: the Small Hunt, which occupies a normal-sized room on the north side of the peristyle, and the Great Hunt, 68 which runs the full length of a 70-metre transversal corridor, off which open some of the most important rooms of the complex. Both are laid out

68 *Detail of the Great Hunt mosaic at Piazza Armerina, Sicily (fourth century* AD*). This 70-metre long corridor mosaic in a luxurious villa represents the hunting and transport of exotic animals for shows in the Roman amphitheatre. The action is displayed, as in African hunt mosaics, with figures and landscape elements at different levels on a neutral white ground. In the foreground a pair of oxen are used to draw a box containing captured animals; in the background beasts of prey attack gazelles.*

in the African manner with independent coloured scenes distributed at different levels on a white ground, and both include numerous details which directly reflect African prototypes. In the Small Hunt is depicted the standard hunting of hares, boar, deer and birds, and many of the episodes, such as the driving of quarry into a netted enclosure, the discovery of a hare hiding in a thicket, and the carrying of a dead boar on a pole (with a dog bounding beneath), are African stereotypes which we have already observed on mosaics from Carthage and El Djem. The Great Hunt shows the collection and transport of exotic beasts for the amphitheatre. Partly rooted in the reality of tropical game-hunts and partly based on popular folklore about the fauna of faraway lands, it is again closely related to African mosaics of similar type, particularly the hunt pavement from Dermech, with which it has in common a number of set pieces: notably a horseman riding with a tiger-cub up the gangplank of a ship, and the use of a baited box to ensnare a beast. It is now, in fact, widely acccepted that both of the Piazza Armerina hunt mosaics, along with most of the others in the villa, were carried out by craftsmen from the Carthage area.

The motif of the polychrome, multi-level big-game hunt has been found in another Sicilian pavement, in a villa on the Tellaro river in the south-east of the island. In this case the composition is much more crowded, and the style of the figures harsher than at Piazza Armerina, and it is less clear that the work was carried out by craftsmen who had come over purposely from Africa. Rather we might think of a 'second-generation' workshop carrying forward the African style in Sicily, or even of local mosaicists who had become proficient in working from Carthaginian pattern-books. This kind of diluted African influence is found in other parts of the Italian peninsula and in the north-western provinces. A hunt mosaic from the Esquiline in Rome, for example, adopts the African com-position of coloured animals and landscape elements scattered over a white ground, and even reproduces the motif of the baited box, but the rendering lacks the fluency and consistency of scale of African work. Although there are occasional instances of close dependence on African patterns – in the fourth-century villa of Desenzano on Lake Garda, for example – the relationship between European mosaics and those of Africa is usually of a very general kind, explicable in terms of the diffusion of patterns and ideas rather than of the direct importation of artists. The hunting scenes on the Lillebonne mosaic are a case in point: the choice of subject, certain motifs such as the sacrifice to Diana, and the use of a neutral white background (though with a faintly suggested terrain at the bottom), all point vaguely to Africa as a source of inspiration, but the mosaicist, as we know from an inscription in the central panel, was from Puteoli (Pozzuoli) in Italy, so the chain of transmission passed through at least one intermediary stage. Hints of African influence which have been detected in British mosaics are of a similar order. The crude chariot-race from Horkstow and a fragment from East Coker (Somerset) with hunters carrying a dead animal on a pole represent remote echoes of the African tradition. Significantly, the East Coker carcass is of a deer, not (as in Africa) a boar.

The one province where more direct African influence is clearly discernible is Spain, separated from Mauretania only by the Straits of Gibraltar. Here not only are there mosaics which employ subject-matter

93

and compositional principles imported from Africa, but also some mosaics so close to African examples as to suggest the hands of immigrant craftsmen. A pair of pavements from the fourth-century villa of El Ramalete near Tudela (Navarre) used a motif of intertwining laurel garlands which is otherwise found only in Africa (in the House of the Trifolium at Dougga, for example). Particularly striking is the taste for the African form of circus mosaic, at least four examples of which have survived in Spain. Those in Barcelona and Gerona provide the same kind of circumstantial detail, with charioteers and horses named, that characterises the documentary mosaics of Africa.

There is, finally, evidence of African infuence even in the eastern Mediterranean, stronghold of *emblema* mosaics. Here it seems that the

new style arrived later than in the West. Though there are hints of it in the fourth-century Hunting and Seasons mosaic from the so-called Constantinian Villa at Daphne, a suburb of Antioch, it is not until the fifth century that we encounter true African-style compositions, with figures scattered freely on a white field which fills the whole of the pavement. The subject-matter *par excellence* in such mosaics was the hunting of exotic animals (whether in the wild or in the amphitheatre), which is depicted on at least half a dozen pavements from Antioch. Once again the currents of transmission were complex, and we should not think of the direct intervention of African workshops, which were in terminal decline in the fifth century, but rather of the late adoption by eastern artists of a style which had ultimately originated in Africa but which had by now become diffused over the whole of the Western Empire. Whatever the truth of the matter, such free-figure mosaics enjoyed a new lease of life in the East in late antiquity. The ultimate seal of approval came with their adoption for the pavements of the peristyle in the imperial palace at Constantinople. Here, probably in the first half of the sixth century, a series of hunting and pastoral scenes, in which individual figures are widely dispersed at different levels against a plain white backdrop, is rendered with a fineness of detail which recalls the *opus vermiculatum* of the Hellenistic period. It would be difficult to imagine a happier marriage of the old pictorial figure style and the new conventions of composition.

69 *Detail of a mosaic pavement in the peristyle of the Great Palace of the Byzantine emperors at Constantinople. The whole of the portico surrounding a court 66.5 m long and 55.5m wide was paved with scenes of hunting and rural life echoing the manner and repertoire of pagan mosaics in North Africa. First half of the sixth century AD.*

69

7 WALL AND VAULT MOSAICS

The tradition of laying floor mosaics continued unabated into the early Christian period. Some of the most extensive and best-preserved mosaic pavements of the ancient world are found in the churches, baptisteries and monasteries of the fifth and sixth centuries, notably in the Near East and North Africa, and at Aquileia and Grado in northern Italy. A spectacular series from Jordan and southern Syria continues even later, into the age of the Ummayad caliphs of the second half of the seventh and the eighth centuries.

In terms of style these mosaics partake of the general tendency of late antique art towards a hardening and flattening of forms, with strong outlines and areas of unmodulated colour; the illusionistic modelling of classical mosaics becomes less and less important. At the same time, again reflecting a general trend of the time, the human figure is usually depicted in frontal aspect, that is in its simplest, most easily comprehensible form. Profile and three-quarter views, together with overlapping and all devices that create effects of recession, are avoided. What matters now is not truth to visual appearances but the clear presentation of a message.

While mythological subjects were still represented in secular buildings as late as the fifth and sixth centuries, the Christian buildings preferred on the whole to avoid human figures. If these occurred, they were personifications (Ktisis or the four rivers of Paradise, for instance), generic figures such as hunters and shepherds, or occasionally representations of the donors who paid for a building to be constructed or a pavement to be laid. Biblical scenes and other overtly Christian subjects were rarely illustrated on floors, at least from the fifth century onwards: there seems to have developed a taboo in regard to treading on sacred images (representations of the 'sign of Christ', presumably the cross or the Christian monogram, were specifically banned by an imperial decree in 427). Much the most popular figural subjects were birds and animals, symbolising the world of nature which God had created and over which He presided, or possibly the paradise which awaited the faithful in an afterlife. Hunted beasts were still represented, for example in some of the late pavements of Antioch already mentioned; but more often we see pacified creatures – sheep, cattle, doves and peacocks – all creatures susceptible of Christian interpretations. Other motifs linked with Christian symbolism, such as fruit-trees, vines and *craters*, were equally popular.

Among the more specialised motifs, found chiefly in the Jordanian series, are inscriptions and representations of buildings and cities. The inscriptions, placed at the threshold of a church or in front of the altar, are incorporated into the decorative scheme by being framed, for example, within the columns of a pedimented façade, or being confronted by a pair of animals, and they often occupy several lines, recording the names of the patron, of the priest or bishop under whose jurisdiction the work took place, and sometimes of the mosaicist himself. The buildings and cities are represented schematically, but often with recognisable elements, such as the Pharos at Alexandria, and with identifying labels. Most elaborate is the vast map of the Holy Land portrayed in the pavement of the church at Madaba, 70 south of Amman. Discovered in 1898, this is sadly damaged, but enough remains to indicate that it covered an area extending from the

70 Jerusalem: detail of a mosaic map of the Holy Land laid in a Byzantine church at Madaba (Jordan). Discovered in the 1890s, this map is now very fragmentary, but it seems originally to have occupied the eastern half of the church and to have measured nearly 16 by 6 metres. Captions in Greek (of which 157 survive) identify individual places. The early Christian mosaics of Syria and Jordan show a marked predilection for topographical representations.

Mediterranean in the west to the Arabian desert in the east, and from Tyre and Sidon in the north to the Nile Delta in the south. It is copiously supplied with labels, naming approximately 150 places, and at the centre, forming a focus, is the walled city of Jerusalem represented in bird's-eye view.

Such motifs are, however, exceptional. The great majority of Christian pavements relied upon geometric ornament, or at the most isolated birds and animals set within the compartments of a repeating pattern. The repertoire of patterns became ever more varied, but all shared a propensity to bright, even garish, use of colour. The 'rainbow style' retained its popularity, especially in the East. Among the favoured repeating patterns were crosses alternating with octagons and elongated hexagons, medallions connected by short bands parallel to the axes of the pavement, and diagonal grids. A

71 *Border of a mosaic pavement in the Umayyad castle at Qasr al-Hallabat (Jordan). In this very late mosaic (eighth century AD) we see motifs from the classical stock, such as the wave-crest, combined with motifs of the late antique period, notably panel frames formed by layered and interlocking 'cables' (a device particularly popular in the Byzantine and Ummayad pavements of Jordan and Syria).*

71 bizarre device, again favoured in the East, but exported from there to western regions such as Spain, was the knotting or intertwining of the frames which defined the decorative scheme. This produced a note of complexity and restlessness alien to the spirit of earlier pavements but wholly in keeping with the rich colorism of this late antique phase.

For all their polychromy, early Christian pavements tended to retain a white background. Much richer in their colouring were the mosaics which now adorned the walls and vaults of churches. It was these wall and vault mosaics that took over the function of displaying major figure subjects. With the vast surfaces available to them, and with no expense spared on time and materials, they came to constitute the greatest achievement of decorators in the fifth and sixth centuries, an achievement that laid the foundations for a tradition continuing far into the medieval period. To put it into context we need to go back in time and trace the origins and evolution of the second main branch of mosaic art.

Wall and vault mosaics have no Hellenistic predecessors. They are an original contribution of the Roman age. Their origins can be traced back to the imitation grottoes, often containing water-sources, which came to be an important feature of Roman Republican villas and gardens. These artificial *nymphaea*, named after the water-nymphs who presided over springs, were encrusted with pumice, marine concretions and varieties of sea-shells to enhance their rustic character; and gradually, as the grottoes took on a more regular architectural shape, their decorations became more formal and made use of a greater variety of materials — marble chippings, pellets of blue frit ('Egyptian blue', a pigment produced by baking a mixture of copper, soda and sand), broken pieces of glass, and ultimately tesserae of both stone and glass. By the beginning of the first century AD this specialised form of mosaic, very different from that of contemporary pavements, had become an established mode of decoration for the walls and vaults of *nymphaea* and similar subterranean rooms. From here developed the use of the term *(opus) museum* or *musivum*. Grottoes were the haunts not just of nymphs but also of the Muses, and the Elder Pliny, writing shortly before his death in AD 79, reveals that structures decorated with pumice 'to look like caves' could be called *musaea*. It seems very likely that this name was transferred from the structures to the type of decoration associated with them, ultimately giving us our term 'mosaic'.

An early example of the new art-form is the decoration of a mid-first-century BC *nymphaeum* in the so-called Villa of Cicero at Formiae, north-west of Naples. Here walls and vaults are coated with pumice and marine concretions, and lines of shells are used to provide further refinement: imitation masonry, pilasters and pavilions on the walls, and coffers in the barrel vault, of an inner recess. This vault decoration is particularly elaborate, with different types of shells, marble chips and blue frit pellets used to reproduce the patterns of contemporary vault decorations in stucco relief. Some of the coffers contain rosettes carried out in reversed mussel shells, others have shields formed by pellets.

Slightly later in date is a vault decoration preserved in the crypto-portico (semi-underground ambula-

72

72 Detail of vault decoration in a nymphaeum *in the so-called Villa of Cicero at Formiae, near Naples: an early example of the incrustation with pumice and marine concretions, marble chippings and shells which led to the emergence of* opus musivum *(wall and vault mosaic). The scheme is inspired by contemporary decorations in stucco relief. Mid-first century BC.*

tory) of a Republican villa incorporated in the later villa of Hadrian at Tivoli. Here there is no pumice: the scheme of concentric square zones enclosing a focal medallion is carried out in white marble chips. Decorative motifs, including garlands, birds and plants, as well as volute and palmette ornaments, are effected partly in pellets of blue frit, partly by differential arrangements of the basic marble chips. Shells are confined to lines along the spring of the vault (oyster) and in the frame of the central roundel (cockle).

73   An early example of a wall mosaic incorporating tesserae is a commemorative plaque in honour of one Gn. Pomponius Hylas from a communal chamber-tomb in the southern part of Rome. Dated to the second quarter of the first century AD, this is framed by a row of cockle-shells (*Cardium edule*) set in red plaster, with a further row of whelk-shells (*Murex brandaris*) above. The epitaph, its wave-crest border and a pair of griffins confronting across a lyre at the bottom are carried out in tesserae of white stone and green, yellow and blue glass, but the background is

73 *Mosaic plaque from the columbarium (communal tomb) of Pomponius Hylas in Rome. Executed in the second quarter of the first century AD, this is one of the earliest examples of a wall mosaic making extensive use of tesserae (in the inscription panel and in the griffins and lyre); but the blue background is formed by pellets of blue frit, the frames by cockle and whelk shells.*

74 *Mosaic-decorated fountain in the House of the Small Fountain at Pompeii. As often at Pompeii and Herculaneum, the play of water was set against a backdrop of wall mosaics. Unlike contemporary floor mosaics, these use coloured backgrounds, and outlines are carried out in shells.*

mainly blue frit, and the line that runs along the inner edge of the frame of cockle-shells is formed by twisted glass rods. The niche that contained the cremated remains of Hylas and his wife had coloured tesserae on the walls and pumice on the semi-dome, with a line of shells along the cornice.

Increased use of tesserae characterises a series of garden fountains built by the householders of Pompeii and Herculaneum in the last generation of life in those cities. These structures, which take the form of a pavilion set against a wall, with a niche from which the water flowed and a crowning pediment, carry decorations which well illustrate the colorism and the new repertory of motifs introduced into wall mosaic during the first century AD. While the lower parts of the walls are coated with pumice (or plates of white marble), and all architectural divisions, as well as the main panel-frames, are defined by rows of shells, the rest of the decoration is executed entirely in tesserae. Unlike the tesserae of contemporary floor mosaics, these are predominantly of glass, which permits the production of bright colours, especially dark blues and greens, but also reds and yellows of a richer hue than can be obtained in stone and terracotta. The polychromy emphasises the affinity of wall mosaics to wall paintings, and many of the motifs which are used – palmettes, candelabra, umbrella canopies, stencil-like borders, and figure subjects such as Venus reclining in a shell, or swans, dolphins and Cupids – are those of contemporary murals. Especially close to paintings are the mosaics of a small courtyard in the House of Neptune and Amphitrite at Herculaneum. On one wall is a fountain niche framed by panels with scenes of dogs hunting deer on a blue ground; on another a panel with the figures of the deities after which the house is named, this time on a yellow ground. In each case the pictures are accompanied by a brilliant play of subsidiary ornament in a full range of colours mimicking the ornament of Pompeian Fourth Style painting.

The imitation of Fourth Style painting is carried much further in a gigantic mosaic wall decoration discovered in 1964 on the north side of the Quirinal hill in Rome. A wall up to five metres in height was entirely covered with a Fourth Style scheme showing almost life-size figures and mythological scenes set amid fantasy architecture in three storeys. Above it, set slightly back, was a semicircular niche which was itself decorated with mosaics. The whole seems to have formed part of a grandiose water display belonging to a private mansion. This chance discovery illustrates how ambitious some compositions in wall mosaic had become by the second

75 *Fountain court in the House of Neptune and Amphitrite at Herculaneum (third quarter of the first century AD). The mosaics here feature figure scenes, dogs hunting deer on the rear wall and the sea-god Neptune with his consort Amphitrite on the right. Much of the subsidiary ornament is closely related to that employed in Fourth Style wall-painting.*

half of the first century and how imperfect is the evidence on which we are forced to assess the progress of the art-form.

It would be wrong, however, to regard wall (and vault) mosaic simply as a more durable substitute for painting. Admittedly, durability must have been one consideration in damp and steamy surroundings such as obtained in fountains and baths, where painted plaster would soon have become mildewed and lost its colour. But more important were the positive aspects of mosaic. The colours provided by glass tesserae were not only unaffected by damp but also much more vivid than those available in the fresco technique; the surface could be regularly wiped clean without suffering harm; and the reflective qualities of the glass would have been particularly attractive in the context of bright light and water. Since the tesserae were not polished smooth as they were in floor mosaics, the myriad varying inclinations of the surface would have created a scintillating effect that no wall painting could rival. The new medium thus acquired its own aesthetic.

The showiness and cost of wall and vault mosaics evidently made them socially desirable. This is demonstrated by the way in which the mosaic fountains in Pompeian gardens were designed to form a focus of attention, often being situated at the end of an axial vista running through the house from the main entrance: when the front door and any intervening doors or partitions were open, visitors would instantly see and admire this manifestation of the householder's fashionable taste. The fountains were frequently built in spaces which were scarcely large enough to accommodate them, so keen were the proprietors to emulate their neighbours. There are also examples of free-standing columns decorated with mosaic, again situated to attract maximum attention. Mosaic vault and wall decorations on a large scale are not attested in the small-town environment of Pompeii; but that wealthier patrons aspired to have them is revealed by their inclusion among the luxurious fittings of private baths described by the Roman moralist Seneca, writing towards AD 64: 'a man feels poor and mean . . . if his vaults are not hidden by glass.' By 'glass' Seneca clearly means glass mosaic. Even allowing for his exaggeration, we can deduce, in the light of the wall mosaics from the Quirinal, that the grandees of the metropolis frequently lavished large sums on providing their houses and villas with decorations in the new mode. The use of vault mosaics in baths presumably copied practice in the great public baths of the capital, such as those built by the emperors Nero and Titus. A comment by Pliny that Agrippa's baths, dedicated in 19 BC, would have had 'glass vaults' if these had been invented surely means that the public baths of his own time had adopted them.

Unfortunately, the vulnerability of walls and vaults means that, after the destruction of Pompeii, very little evidence remains of the mosaics which once adorned them. However, there are sufficient discoveries of loose glass tesserae or impressions of tesserae in the plaster of standing structures to indicate the former existence of such mosaics in many buildings of the Imperial age, especially public baths and palaces. Numerous traces survive, for example, in Hadrian's villa at Tivoli, in the Baths of Caracalla, and in the so-called Baths (perhaps part of an imperial palace) in the thermal resort of Baiae, near Naples. All these were vault decorations, and most come from lofty halls where the original effect must have been magnificent; it is sad that we can gain no real conception of their colour and design. It is not until the late third century that we have a half-complete vault decoration, and this is a small-scale specimen from a tomb. The mausoleum of the Julii (Tomb M) in the necropolis under the later basilica of St Peter's in Rome provides the first example of mosaic used for Christian imagery. In the centre of the vault, on a yellow ground which surprisingly foreshadows the luminous gold backgrounds of the Byzantine period, we see a charioteer and his team of horses amid a tracery of vine tendrils. The head of the charioteer is nimbed and surrounded by rays that

76

indicate that he is the sun-god Sol; but the accompanying scenes on the upper parts of the walls, which include a representation of the Good Shepherd and the story of Jonah and the whale, show that we are dealing with a Christian programme. The sun-god is here assimilated with the risen Christ, source of light and salvation. The owners who commissioned the (secondary) decoration of this small tomb were clearly adherents of the new faith that was destined to conquer the Roman world, and, like many of their fellow believers, they were happy to have Christian ideas expressed through the medium of familiar pagan images.

Two great complexes of vault mosaics from the fourth century show a similar fusion of pagan and Christian. The first is the mausoleum of the emperor Constantine's daughter Constantina, now the

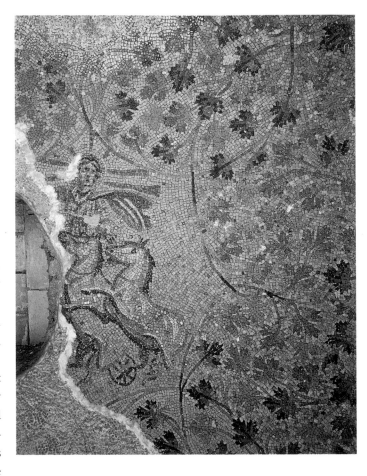

76 *Mosaic vault decoration of mausoleum M in the necropolis under St Peter's basilica in the Vatican City, Rome. The mosaic, which belongs to a late third-century redecoration of an earlier tomb, shows a charioteer with rays emerging from his head in the manner of depictions of the sun-god Sol; but the presence of Christian subjects on the walls suggests that Sol is here identified with Christ.*

church of Santa Costanza in Rome. This is a circular building with a central domed space ringed by a barrel-vaulted corridor. The mosaics of the central dome were destroyed in 1620, but drawings of the fifteenth and sixteenth centuries give us a good idea of the original scheme, the main part of which consisted of twelve narrow sectors separated by elaborate vegetal candelabra containing caryatids (female supporting figures). While these candelabra and a zone round the base of the dome which showed marine subjects, including aquatic birds, sea-creatures and Cupids fishing from boats, are derived from the standard classical repertoire, the spaces between the candelabra contained biblical scenes in two tiers – subjects from the Old Testament below (including Susanna and the Elders, the sacrifice of Cain and Abel, and Moses striking the rock) and subjects from the New Testament above (to judge from the only one recorded, the healing of the centurion). In contrast with the dome, the mosaics in the vault of the surrounding corridor are pagan in subject and rooted in the tradition of floor mosaics rather than vault mosaics. The decoration, well preserved (though heavily restored in the nineteenth century), is divided into eleven successive rectangular sections, each of which has a white background and carries a composition (in reds, yellows, blues and greens) familiar from the repertoire of mosaic pavements. There are four geometric patterns: the familiar late antique system of crosses alternating with octagons and elongated hexagons, a scheme of lozenges arranged point to point at right angles so as to form four-point stars in the interstices, a pattern of bands which intertwine to form large medallions containing figures of Cupids and Psyches and concave-sided octagons containing animals and birds, and a pattern of tangent medallions containing small figures (again Cupids and Psyches), busts and floral motifs. More remarkable are the free-figure compositions, which find their closest parallels in the pavements of North Africa. Two show an overall decoration of sprawling vine tendrils with vintaging putti accompanied, at the spring of the vault, by scenes of the transport and treading of the grapes; the general decorative formula and the interest in depicting rustic labours are characteristics found in various African pavements, for example at Cherchel. The remaining two compositions, each of which consists of scattered fruit-branches, birds and silver 77 vessels, are clearly related to the pavements of strewn foliage which we have noted at Carthage. It is odd to find these subjects on a vault rather than a pavement, but, given the loss of almost every other vault decoration of the period, it is difficult to judge how far the treatment was really exceptional.

The second major fourth-century vault decoration comes from another circular mausoleum, this time at Centcelles, near Tarragona in Spain. While the mausoleum has been linked with another member of Constantine's family, his son Constans I, who died on his way to Spain in 350, there is no conclusive evidence in favour of this theory and it is best to keep an open mind. All we can say is that the grand scale of the dome and the richness of its mosaics point to a patron of no mean wealth and standing. More or less extensive fragments of the mosaics survive *in situ*. Unfortunately the central roundel, which might have provided a clue to the ownership of the mausoleum and the complex of buildings associated with it, is lost apart from a couple of heads belonging to unidentified figures. Round this ran three broad figured zones. Proceeding outwards from the centre, the first one contained figures representing the four Seasons and four scenes of uncertain meaning, each of which consisted of an enthroned figure in ceremonial robes with three to four figures standing in attendance. The second zone contained a series of sixteen biblical scenes, including Adam and Eve, Daniel in the lions' den, the story of Jonah (in three episodes), the Good Shepherd (emphasised by being placed directly

opposite the entrance), Noah and the ark, the raising of Lazarus, and the three Hebrews in the fiery furnace. The final zone showed successive stages of a deer-hunt in the standard tradition first seen in Africa. These figure zones are separated, and the individual panels framed, by rich polychrome ornament in tones of red, yellow, green and blue, including confronting S-volutes and a scale pattern; their backgrounds are in some cases white, in others coloured. The backgrounds in the throne scenes are of gold in the upper half and light green below, and that in the central roundel entirely gold. Whoever the person buried in this mausoleum, he clearly shared the taste for hunting characteristic of the landed aristocracy of the period, and like many of his contemporaries he had embraced the Christian faith whilst retaining a learned attachment to classical mythology (Autumn is personified by a figure of Dionysus).

Though we have talked of pagan elements in these fourth-century mosaics, it is perhaps better to use the term 'profane'. The predominant

77 Detail of the vault of the circular corridor round the mausoleum of Constantina (now the church of Santa Costanza) in Rome. This section shows scattered fruit-branches, birds and vessels, a decorative convention found first in the pavements of Africa. Second quarter of the fourth century AD.

emphasis outside the Christian scenes is on hunting and wine-production, which are of course neutral in their meaning; they refer, like the ceremonial scenes at Centcelles, to the dead man's status. Such pagan motifs as occur are used in a conventional way, either as convenient metaphors (thus the Cupids and Psyches in Santa Costanza possibly symbolised the souls of the dead) or simply out of deference to a long-standing decorative tradition. The mosaics of the two mausolea are essentially Christian, and as such they stand at the threshold of the great series of Christian wall and vault mosaics which extends into the Middle Ages.

The surviving remains of wall and vault mosaics become abundant from the late fourth century onwards. While the secular buildings of earlier centuries were allowed to fall into ruins or were destroyed, the Christian churches of the new era have been maintained and restored down to the present day, so that their decorations are often miraculously complete. The subject-matter of these decorations dispenses with all pagan and profane elements. Given that the buildings in question had a purely religious function, and that a more vigorous anti-pagan attitude was introduced under the emperor Theodosius I (379-95), the dominance of Christian iconography is hardly surprising. Only a few selected examples need be mentioned. In Italy the chapel of St Aquilinus in the church of San Lorenzo Maggiore in Milan has an apse mosaic of the late fourth 78 century in which Christ is shown centrally, teaching the twelve apostles, who are standing in groups of six at each side, all on a neutral gold ground. The baptistery of San Giovanni in Fonte in Naples has a dome mosaic of the early fifth century in which an elaborate decoration incorporating

78 *Apse of the chapel of St Aquilinus in the church of San Lorenzo Maggiore, Milan. Christ, with nimbed head, is shown as a teacher, a basket of scrolls at his feet, amid the twelve Apostles. The background above the figures' heads uses the gold tesserae much favoured in early Christian mosaics.*

drapes, birds and fruit garlands welds together different themes from the New Testament, all on a dark blue ground. The basilica of Santa Maria Maggiore in Rome, constructed between 432 and 440, preserves wall mosaics in the nave, beneath the clerestory windows and on the triumphal arch (the wall through which the apse is extruded), showing respectively Old Testament scenes and stories of Christ's childhood. Here the backgrounds are predominantly blue and green, but contain a certain amount of gold. In the East, the church of Hagios Georgios in Thessaloniki, decorated around 400, preserves mosaics in the lower part of its dome, with elaborate architectural structures serving as a backdrop for depictions of various saints, all on a gold ground.

Many of the finest wall and vault mosaics of this early Christian phase were applied in Ravenna, which succeeded Milan as the capital of the Western Empire in the fifth century. The little mausoleum of Galla Placidia (440-50), which has a cruciform plan, is decorated all over its barrel vaults, central dome and lunettes with mosaics in which blue and gold predominate; the vaults carry vegetal or floral designs, and the dome a large cross, while figure subjects are reserved for the lunettes (the Good Shepherd above the entrance, St Lawrence at the back of the far recess, and pairs of apostles under the dome). In the Baptistery of the Orthodox, a perfectly 79 preserved dome mosaic executed soon after 450 shows the baptism of Christ with gold ground in a central roundel, and the twelve apostles standing between candelabra on a blue ground in an encircling zone. In the church of San Vitale, begun in the 520s, the apse has Christ seated on a celestial globe between a pair of angels, with St Vitalis on the left and the archbishop Ecclesius, builder of the church, on the right; the vault of the presbytery carries an elaborate decoration of scrolls focused upon a roundel containing the Lamb supported by four angels; and two mosaic panels added to the walls of the apse when Ravenna came under Byzantine rule in 540 show the emperor Justinian and his empress 80 Theodora in company with officials, soldiers and ladies of the court on a golden ground. Here mother-of-pearl has been used alongside the standard glass tesserae to enrich the crowns and jewellery of the imperial couple.

The mosaics of Ravenna mark the culmination of the evolution of wall and vault mosaic which began with the first tentative shell and pumice incrustation of late Republican *nymphaea*. At the same time they embody the new spirit of representational art in the late antique period. Scrolls and vegetal elements are reduced to strictly formal patterns; figures stand stiff and in frontal view, often with elongated proportions; colours are strong and outlined by solid dark contours. The figure style is, to some extent,

dictated by the grand scale of many of the churches: bold colours and clear outlines take cognisance of the distance from which the figures have to be seen, and the elongated proportions are designed partly to counteract the optical distortion created by the low vantage point of the viewer, especially when figures were applied to the curved surfaces of vaults and domes. But there are also ideological factors at work. We are now dealing with an art which is intended not to entertain but to instruct – with figures which are not involved in a self-contained world remote from reality but which are meant to address the worshipper directly. The result is a style that rejects the refined illusionism, complex movement and carefully graded colours of the early figure panels depicted in Hellenistic pavements. Like sculpture and painting, mosaic has passed from its classical phase to the hieratic mode of the Byzantine era. It was to be another thousand years before the wheel turned full circle and artists once more sought to capture the pictorial illusions achieved in the Graeco-Roman age.

80 Theodora and her retinue: mosaic panel in the apse of San Vitale, Ravenna. Justinian's empress is shown symbolically coming to the basilica bearing gifts (c. AD 547). On the opposite wall a similar panel showed Justinian himself accompanied by the archbishop Maximianus and members of his clergy. Neither Justinian nor Theodora ever visited Ravenna.

8 CONTEXT AND MEANING

81 Aeneid *mosaic from Low Ham (Somerset) in Britain, now in Taunton Castle Museum. The scenes narrate the story of Dido and Aeneas, best known from books i and iv of Virgil's* Aeneid, *in anticlockwise sequence. An ancient viewer could have walked round the room to follow the narrative, but the museum display sets the pavement vertically, and even turns the central scene upside down.*

So far we have looked at ancient mosaics chiefly in formal terms, reviewing patterns, motifs and subject-matter in relation to their artistic development. It is essential, however, to remember that they formed part of a real world of buildings and people. They were applied to architectural surfaces, often at great expense, by patrons who usually had to live with them and who may have wanted to express particular ideas through them. It is important, therefore, to put them in context. By looking at their relation to the spaces in which they were displayed and at the social roles that they fulfilled we may gain a deeper understanding of ancient mosaics and their meaning.

The architectural setting is of paramount importance. While many wall and vault mosaics, especially those of early Christian churches, but also those of the garden fountains in Pompeii and Herculaneum, can still be

seen much as they were intended, floor mosaics are frequently displayed in conditions which to a greater or lesser degree falsify their original effect. In museums it is rarely possible to set them on the floor; they are usually attached to walls, with the result that the viewer sees them head on, and crucial details, as in the *Aeneid* mosaic from Low Ham 81 exhibited in the Castle Museum at Taunton in Britain, are upside down. The same happens when mosaics are illustrated in books: photographs normally show them square on, like works hung in a gallery. No viewer in antiquity would have confronted a mosaic in this way. He or she would have seen it from above, at an oblique angle, with certain viewpoints privileged by the position of doorways and certain areas obscured by furniture. At the same time, he or she could walk over it, establishing a personal relationship with it and appreciating it from different positions. All this is lost in the modern museum exhibition. Even where there is space to display a mosaic pavement on the floor (like the Hinton St Mary mosaic in the British Museum), the viewer is rarely allowed to walk over it. It is usually raised above floor-level and roped off, forcing the museum visitor to walk round it and view it from the exterior – something which would have been impossible in antiquity because the walls of the room would have been in the way! As a vivid illustration of the artificiality of such displays, the Hunting and Seasons pavement from Daphne, now in the Louvre, has actually been doctored to take account of the position of the modern spectator: the panels along the margins of the pavement, originally oriented to face the centre, have been turned to face outwards.

Where mosaic pavements are preserved *in situ* on archaeological sites, the contextualisation is obviously more satisfactory; but there are still anomalies. Visitors are usually unable to walk over them, but must view them from a distance. The walls around them seldom stand more than a few courses high, if they survive at all, so that it is impossible to experience the original lighting conditions, or indeed sometimes even to know where doors or windows were situated. And once again we see the mosaic from the outside looking in rather than from the inside looking out.

It requires an effort of the imagination, therefore, to set mosaic pavements in their architectural context. Something will be said shortly about

82 *Remains of a Roman house (first century AD) at Ampurias (Spain): a typical view of mosaic pavements on an archaeological site. Visitors are not allowed to walk on the mosaics, and must look at them from the exterior, over the truncated remnants of the walls which would originally have enclosed and hidden them. The viewpoint and lighting thus give a totally false impression of the ancient appearance.*

the ways in which they relate to that context. First we need to summarise the types of buildings, and the kind of rooms within these buildings, in which they occurred.

In theory mosaics could be laid in all kinds of buildings, public and private. In Greek times we find them in at least two royal palaces (at Vergina in Macedonia, and at Pergamum) and in temples (the temple of Zeus at Olympia and the temple of Despoina at Lycosura). In Roman times they occur in a number of different types of public buildings, especially bath buildings (the Baths of Caracalla in Rome, for instance, and the municipal baths at Pompeii, Herculaneum and Ostia), before becoming a standard medium for the decoration of early Christian churches, both in pavements and on walls and vaults. But for pavements, at least, mosaic came second in the scale of prestige to *opus sectile*. Especially after the expansion of the trade in coloured stones during the early Imperial period it became normal to endow major public buildings with pavements in this technique (just as their walls were frequently adorned with marble veneers, displacing painting). Mosaic was thus left principally in the hands of private patrons. The vast majority of mosaic pavements throughout the Greek and Roman age derive from private buildings, and especially from houses.

The extent to which mosaics were laid in houses varied from period to period and from place to place. We have seen how the incidence of mosaics increased in Hellenistic times, until a relatively large proportion of rooms in the houses of Delos had them, and how the extent to which houses in Roman North Africa were paved with mosaics was far greater than in other parts of the Roman world (of known sites, only Antioch offers a comparable density). But it is possible to get a false or exaggerated impression of the prevalence of mosaics. There were other types of decorative and durable pavements, such as *opus signinum* (with or without patterns of spaced tesserae) and various forms of *terrazzo* paving. Interesting statistics compiled for one region in Pompeii revealed that only 2.5 per cent of the floors were paved with mosaics and that 75 per cent of these mosaics were concentrated in only three houses. Even in North Africa there were modest houses that lacked mosaics, and those houses that were extensively decorated with mosaics did not have them in certain rooms. In other parts of the Roman world the houses that had numerous rooms decorated with mosaics were exceptional; the general rule was that only a few rooms were singled out in this way.

Where mosaics occurred in several rooms, there was a clear grading in terms of importance. The same grading has been observed in wall paintings, where it has been recognised as representing a sliding scale of prices charged to the client by the firm of decorators. At the top of the scale, in both paintings and mosaics, would have been those that were most expensive of time and materials, namely decorations involving a rich variety of colours and featuring mythological figure scenes. In mosaics the next stage down the scale would have been represented by coloured pavements with minor figure subjects, such as animals and birds, and those with floral and geometric patterns. Below these would have come geometric compositions of reduced complexity and limited colours, then increasingly simple patterns in black and white, and finally plain tessellation.

The most expensive pavements, naturally, were used in the largest and most important rooms, notably rooms in which visitors were received. Pre-eminent among these were the *oeci* (saloons) and dining-rooms, which are normally the largest of all and are set in privileged positions, commanding a view into a garden, for example, or located so as to be remote from the noise of streets and the disturbance of household activities. Also singled out were the guest bedrooms and the special bedroom or sitting-room in which the householder received favoured friends and clients. Another favoured zone was the domestic bath suite, where not only the family but also invited guests would have benefited from a luxury that was confined to the affluent classes (lesser householders would have had to frequent the public baths). Bedrooms and bathrooms tended to receive less elaborate mosaics than the main reception rooms, but were still relatively high on the scale. Rather simpler decorations were reserved for the subsidiary spaces, including rooms of passage – those spaces through which visitors passed to reach the prime reception zones.

There was, of course, a vast range of variations upon this basic formula, and the absolute position of given mosaics within the scale of elaboration depended upon the spending power of the patron. The less money he had, the fewer figure mosaics he could afford – and the more cheaply produced were those that he did commission. By and large, however, the ideal at most periods was to have figure mosaics in dining-rooms and *oeci*, and if possible in bedrooms and bathrooms too, while non-figured patterns were assigned mainly to subsidiary rooms. This choice reflects not only the relative importance but also the nature of the rooms. Figure mosaics tend to impose specific viewpoints and to demand contemplation. They were thus best suited to rooms into which people looked, or within which they spent time. Floral or geometric patterns, on the other hand, impose no single viewpoint and are capable of endless extension. They were thus preferred for rooms of passage, where they led the eye onwards and presented no focus on which viewers would be tempted to linger. A similar distinction of treatment is observable in wall paintings: centralised schemes, often with a mythological picture panel, were applied in rooms of rest, and paratactic or repeating schemes, in which there was no single focus, in rooms of passage.

Good examples of these principles at work can be seen in certain villas in Roman Britain. In the main building of the villa at Brading, Isle of Wight, there was a figure mosaic showing Orpheus and the beasts directly inside the main doorway, providing the newly arrived visitor with an immediate focus of interest. To left and right of this, however, a plain chequerboard mosaic led him or her onwards, without distraction, to the main show rooms in the wings – a bedroom at the south and a bipartite dining-room at the north, each of which had figure mosaics which invited leisurely study. Similar arrangements are found in the villa at Bignor, Sussex, where most of the mosaics were concentrated in a suite at the north-west corner. Here the two largest and most distinctive rooms, the bipartite room 7 and the apsidal room 3, were marked out by the use of figure mosaics, showing respectively Ganymede borne off by Jupiter in the guise of an eagle and a bust of a goddess (Venus?) together with a whimsical frieze of Cupids dressed as gladiators. The passage 6, on the other hand, had a floral and geometric mosaic, and the long corridor 10 one with an endlessly repeated meander pattern.

Not only did mosaics differentiate between one room and another; they also served to differentiate space within a room. At the simplest level

83

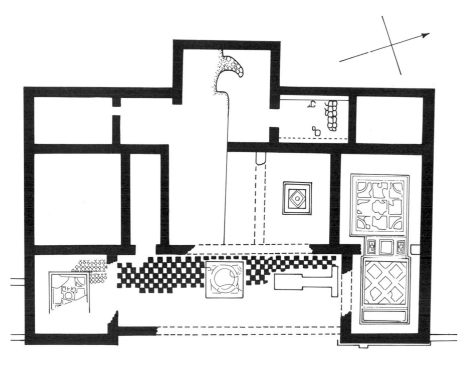

83 *Plan of the main residential building of the villa at Brading (Isle of Wight), Britain. The position and form of the mosaics reinforce the functions of spaces within the house: a mythological panel greets visitors as they enter the main doorway, then a plain chequerboard pavement leads them left or right to two important rooms with further mythological pavements – a dining-room in the north wing and a bedroom in the south.*

a mosaic panel frequently marked out the threshold. If there were colonnades, as happened in certain types of *oecus*, the intercolumniations were filled with mosaic panels which provided a kind of visual stylobate (foundation course) and thus bound the columns together, but which also reinforced the functional divisions between the central space and the side aisles. In bedrooms the position of beds was often defined by differences in pattern and by a narrow dividing band decorated with various forms of geometric or vegetal ornament – a band called by Italian writers *scendiletto* (literally 'place for getting out of bed'). In dining-rooms a similar dividing band differentiated the back third of the room, where the dining-couches were situated, from the front two thirds, which functioned as a service area (and no doubt sometimes also as a place for post-prandial floor-shows). Generally speaking, the parts of a room which were expected to be hidden by furniture, such as the beds in a bedroom and the dining-couches in a dining-room, were left plain or decorated with simple geometric patterns. More elaborate patterns or figure scenes were placed in the unobstructed areas.

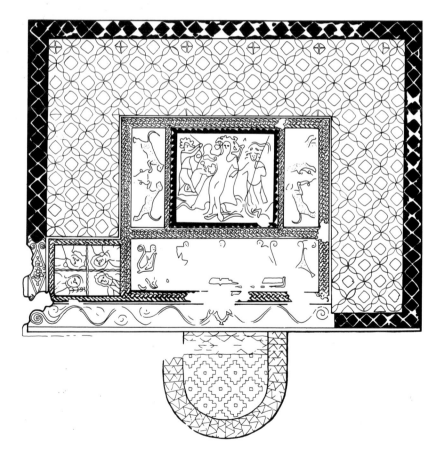

84 *Diagram of a pavement in a dining-room in the House of Bacchus at Alcalá de Henares, near Madrid (late fourth or early fifth century AD). The simple geometrically decorated area indicates the position of the dining-couches, while the figure subjects, representing the wine-god Dionysus and his drunken retinue, together with busts of the four Seasons, occupy the spaces which would have been left visible to the banqueters.*

85 *Jupiter, disguised as a bull, abducts Europa: detail of a pavement in the villa at Lullingstone, Kent. The mosaic, which is set in the apse of a dining-room, is oriented to face the diners, seated around it on a semicircular couch. Above the scene is an inscription in Latin elegiacs: 'If jealous Juno had seen the swimming of the bull, more justly would she have repaired to the halls of Aeolus.' This alludes to Juno's mission to the god of the winds in the first book of Virgil's* Aeneid.

As time went on, the arrangements for marking out space in dining-rooms became increasingly elaborate. The design of the pavement often took the form of the Greek character pi (Π) interlocking with an inverted T. The pi, which would have been hidden by the typical arrangement of three couches (*triclinium*), was decorated simply, or not at all, while the T, which remained visible, carried figure scenes and the like. Good illustrations are furnished by the dining-room pavements in the Atrium House at Antioch and the House of Aion at Paphos, both mentioned in Chapter 4. The same arrangement is seen in a dining-room from a villa at Alcalá de Henares near Madrid, where the position of the dining-couches 84 was marked by a diagonal grid pattern, while the visible part of the floor carried Dionysiac scenes. Later still, as a continuous semicircular couch (*stibadium*) tended to supplant the three-couch *triclinium*, this was indicated by semicircular divisions in the mosaic pavement. At Lullingstone (Kent, 85 in Britain), for example, a broad horseshoe-shaped area of plain red tessellation marked the position of the couch, and a semicircular panel containing a depiction of the myth of Europa and the bull occupied the remaining space.

The orientation of figure scenes within a pavement varied. Normally, where there was a single entrance, the main figural elements faced the doorway, so that they would be seen by someone entering or looking into the room; but in several dining- and sitting-rooms, like the *exedra* with the amphora and palm-branch in the House of the Trident on Delos (Chapter 2), they were turned towards viewers at the rear. In the Lullingstone dining-room just mentioned, for example, the Europa scene and a verse inscription which accompanied it were designed to be seen by diners on the *stibadium*. In the House of the Drinking Contest at Antioch the scene

36   which gives the house its name was turned towards the rear couch in a *triclinium*. In those rooms where no beds or couches were expected to obstruct the pavement, and the figural elements accordingly extended to the walls, the outer scenes normally faced inwards for the benefit of a viewer in the middle: thus the original orientation of the scenes at the edges of the Hunting and Seasons mosaic from Daphne. The situation changed radically, however, where a room had more than one entrance. In such cases it was felt desirable to switch the orientation of the figures to accommodate a number of different viewpoints. This was part of the rationale underlying the arrangement of figures in the black and white

27, 30 marine mosaics of the baths at Ostia (Chapter 3), and it also accounts for the way in which the scenes of rustic labours in the central field of the pavement at Oudna mentioned in Chapter 6 turn the corners to face the sides. In each case the objective was to provide at least one element which was correctly oriented for a person entering the room from a different direction. It would also have been possible for the viewer to follow the action round the room as he or she proceeded from one doorway to another.

Interesting questions are raised by the relationship between the themes employed in mosaics and the functions of the spaces that they decorated. Here, leaving aside religious buildings (temples, synagogues and churches), where the imagery was almost invariably chosen from the relevant religious repertoire, the most obvious links are in bath suites, where mosaicists regularly depicted themes associated with water, particularly the marine

27   cortège of sea-horses, sea-bulls, sea-centaurs and Tritons, with sea-nymphs, Cupids and swimming dolphins in attendance, which accompanied the sea-god Neptune and his consort Amphitrite. Since baths were also associated with physical exercise, an alternative theme was the world of athletics, as illustrated by the figures of athletes in an apsidal mosaic from the Baths of Caracalla in Rome. In other types of rooms links between theme and function are less common than might be expected. In dining-rooms, for instance, while there are many pavements with clear references

to wining and dining (the drinking contest of Dionysus and Heracles at Antioch, general Dionysiac figures and scenes in Alcalá de Henares and Cologne, and most strikingly a horseshoe-shaped table laden with food directly in front of the *stibadium* couch in the House of the Buffet Supper at Daphne), the references are often of a vaguer order (still lifes of food, or simply pictures of birds and animals) or of no direct relevance at all. Many dining-rooms were decorated with general subjects from heroic legend or romantic myth (the story of Europa and the bull at Lullingstone, for example); here the only explanation can be that they were designed to entertain the diners by appealing to their love of classical literature and to a taste for learned allusion (the verse inscription above the Europa panel at Lullingstone presupposes a knowledge of the first book of Virgil's *Aeneid*). It is possible also that such stories were the subject of recitations, or even of dramatic performances, that were staged in the dining-room after the meal.

33, 36
84

85

In bedrooms the range of subjects was more heterogeneous. Some, such as representations of Venus and Cupid, and amorous encounters of satyrs and bacchantes, might seem appropriate enough; but the majority of subjects are chosen from the standard mythological stock. Personal taste, often of a seemingly arbitrary kind, clearly bulked larger than any desire to make the theme match the setting.

86 *Fragment of a pavement with a scene of Selene and Endymion. This black and white mosaic from a tomb in the necropolis of the imperial port of Rome, near Ostia, depicts a subject appropriate to the funerary context: the young huntsman's eternal sleep and the sanctity conferred by the visits of the moon-goddess provide a paradigm of death as a blessed state.*

One particular type of building where interior decorations, including mosaic pavements, sometimes incorporated subjects relevant to the function was the funerary monument. Not many such monuments actually had mosaics, but there were four or five examples in chamber-tombs in Rome which showed the seizure of Persephone by the Underworld god Pluto (Hades), an apt metaphor for death, and one which offered some hope of a future existence, since Persephone was eventually granted terms which allowed her to spend six months each year back on earth. A similar idea is involved in a mosaic from a tomb in the necropolis of Isola Sacra near Ostia, where we see Alcestis rescued from the Underworld

by Heracles. Another funerary mosaic from Isola Sacra carried a depiction
86 of the moon-goddess Selene visiting the sleeping huntsman Endymion –
a subject that once again symbolised death but made it seem less final and
forbidding: Endymion's eternal sleep was turned into a kind of apotheosis
by the goddess's love. Like the rape of Persephone, the union of Selene
and Endymion was a favourite motif in funerary art, appearing frequently
in the carved reliefs on sarcophagi. Yet another mosaic from Isola Sacra
refers to death in a more specific and starker fashion by depicting the
ferryman Charon rowing the deceased across the water which marks the
boundary of the Underworld. But not every motif in the decoration of
tombs was equally appropriate. A fourth mosaic at Isola Sacra shows the
nine Muses. It is difficult to understand how this subject could be regarded
as especially pertinent to a sepulchral context: like many of the subjects in
tomb-paintings and in the reliefs on funerary altars or cinerary urns, not to
mention sarcophagi, the reason for its selection escapes us.

So far we have looked at the mosaic medium largely in isolation, but it
was of course only one of a number of media which often shared or
exchanged ideas. Textiles, for example, may have exerted some influence
on mosaics. Unfortunately, few ancient textiles survive except in fragments,
and we have no information about the existence or otherwise of woven
floor-coverings. Indeed, the widespread use of mosaic and other kinds of
decorative paving implies that such coverings were not a regular feature:
there would have been no point in laying a mosaic if it was to be hidden
by a carpet. But we have more than once noticed the resemblances
87 between mosaics and woven fabrics. The 'rainbow style' in particular, with

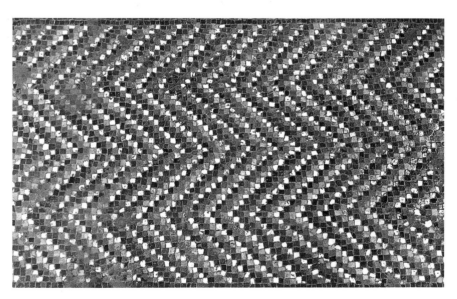

87 *Zigzag motif in the
'rainbow style': detail of
a pavement in the House
of the Hunt at Bulla
Regia (Tunisia). The
pattern of tesserae
changing colour along the
diagonal is reminiscent of
the effect of woven cloth,
and may possibly
illustrate the influence of
textiles upon mosaics.*

its diagonal settings and tessera by tessera colour changes, produces effects remarkably similar to those of the interweaving threads in textiles. It is not inconceivable that a pavement such as that of Ananeosis at Antioch owed some inspiration to draperies used in interior decoration – perhaps curtains and other hangings if not actual woven floor-coverings.

The most obvious relationship, however, is between mosaic and painting, since many mosaic panels, notably the *emblemata* of Hellenistic times, were based upon paintings whose illusionistic treatment they faithfully copied. An extreme example is the Alexander mosaic from Pompeii, whose 16 complex figure composition could never have been conceived without a painted prototype, presumably a famous masterpiece of the early Hellenistic period. In some cases mosaic panels of this pictorial type were set in walls, occupying the position traditionally reserved for paintings: a recent study has grouped together various mosaic *emblemata* of the second and third centuries AD, most of which were found out of context, and established that they were probably made for walls rather than floors. One of them, showing the death of Pentheus, torn apart by his mother and her fellow bacchantes, is still *in situ* in the wall of a tomb in the necropolis under St Peter's. It is possible, too, that the famous mosaic portrait of a 88 woman from a house at Pompeii may originally have been set in a wall, though its ultimate position was in the middle of a pavement.

The imitation by mosaics of paintings is an obvious form of dependence; but there was also a more general level at which exchange of ideas took place – namely in the sharing of compositional types. Ancient art relied heavily upon the transmission of stock iconographic formulae to present stories: a particular mythological episode would come to be associated with a particular composition, particular gestures and particular attributes, enabling the trained viewer to read it as a kind of visual language, without the need for labels. As we saw in Chapter 4, eastern mosaicists and painters at first used labels only where they thought their pictures might not otherwise be understood (though later the addition of labels became a more regular practice, whether from convention or because visual 'literacy' had actually declined). Thus at Paphos the story of Poseidon and Amymone was recognisable from the god's trident, the 89 nymph's jug and their respective postures (amorous advance and alarmed retreat); these visual clues were used repeatedly in representations of the episode, and the well-informed viewer would have had no difficulty in reading the scene. Such standard formulae were in use for a wide variety of mythological themes and their occurrence in a mosaic does not necessarily indicate copying of a specific painted prototype: they have become the common stock in trade of both mosaicists and painters. And not just

88 *Female portrait from Pompeii, now in Naples, National Museum. Though found in the centre of a pavement of opus sectile, this famous panel (25.5 × 20.5 cm) was perhaps originally set in a wall. The absence of any distinguishing attributes rules out identification as a figure from mythology, so the bust probably represents an anonymous private individual.*

mosaicists and painters – the same types are found in other media, such as relief sculpture. The iconographic formula for the triumph of Dionysus
59 seen in several North African mosaics, for instance, is related to a formula used in sarcophagus reliefs in Rome. Compositional schemes formed part of a standard iconographic repertory that could be quoted by artists in different media.

In addition to reproducing well-known panel paintings, and to sharing a common stock of iconographic types, mosaic showed the influence of painting in a number of other ways. This is most clear in wall mosaics,

89 *Poseidon (Neptune) and Amymone. Detail of a mosaic pavement in the House of Dionysus at Paphos, Cyprus (late second or early third century AD). Whereas other adjacent panels contain labels to identify the figures, this scene was considered sufficiently well known for viewers to identify the subjects from visual clues: the god's trident, the nymph's jug, and the two figures' respective poses.*

which frequently echo the colours and compositions of wall paintings. A Second Style painted scheme, for example, inspires the early pumice and shell mosaic on the side walls of the inner recess of the *nymphaeum* at Formiae, and a Fourth Style scheme is reproduced in the huge wall mosaic found to the north of the Quirinal in Rome. More general use of the ornamental borders and stock figures of Fourth Style wall-painting is attested in the mosaic decoration of garden fountains at Pompeii and Herculaneum. Fourth Style borders appear also on fragments of wall mosaic retrieved from a pair of pleasure-boats scuttled in Lake Nemi in central Italy. But mural paintings are also reflected on pavements. Most striking is a group of mosaics from Antioch, dated to the early third century, in which mythological subjects are framed in architectural structures directly borrowed from the standard repertory of wall-painting and represented in precisely the same way: the perspective and shading presuppose the head-on viewpoint of a spectator looking at a wall and seem positively out of place on a floor.

Floor decoration not surprisingly shows a much closer relationship to the decoration of ceilings than to that of walls. Here we are not thinking just of paintings. Ceilings were decorated in various media (wooden panelling, stucco relief, painting and eventually mosaic), and these influenced each other in a complex and changing interplay of ideas, so that it is often difficult to know which particular source or combination of sources accounts for a composition used in a given pavement. But certain examples provide clear pointers. That the coffered patterns of many mosaic pavements in Italy during the first century BC were based upon wooden ceilings and upon the stucco vault decorations that were themselves derived

74-5

36

22

from these wooden ceilings is beyond dispute. Even some of the more complex patterns which appear in late Republican pavements may have been inspired by stucco work. The liberating effect of the curved surface of the vault led stuccoists to break free from the constraints of square or rectangular coffers and to develop a number of new patterns based on diagonal grids, hexagons, lozenges and medallions; many of the same patterns first appeared in mosaic pavements about the same time, and it is now generally acknowledged that it was from stucco vaults that the mosaicists drew their inspiration.

In Imperial times we find occasional references to vaults in more general structural terms. Most specific is the central part of a mosaic pavement in the House of the Boat of Psyches at Daphne, where a scene of Europa and the bull is framed by a couple of superimposed cornices with pairs of projecting brackets, a mask on the lower one supporting the one above.

90 Europa and the bull: centrepiece of a mosaic pavement in the House of the Boat of Psyches at Antioch, now in Baltimore. The elaborate perspectival border with masks appearing to support a jutting cornice is a motif appropriate to the top of a wall and leads the viewer to think that he or she is looking up at a ceiling. Third century AD.

91 *Dionysiac mosaic from the House of Bacchus at Djemila (Cuicul) in Algeria (second or third quarter of the second century AD). The various scenes depict episodes from the mythology and ritual of Dionysus; at the centre is Lycurgus, driven mad by Dionysus for persecuting the god. The layout of the mosaic, with caryatids on the diagonals, suggests a design inspired by a decorated cross-vault.*

The perspective, centralised on each side, is purposely designed to suggest that the viewer is looking up at a ceiling. Several pavements, including the *frigidarium* mosaic in the Baths of Neptune at Acholla, the Cartdrivers mosaic at Ostia, the Hunting and Seasons mosaic from Daphne, and a famous Dionysiac mosaic at Djemila (Cuicul) in Algeria, have designs which place strong emphasis upon the diagonals, recalling the groined cross-vaults which are a dominant feature of Imperial architecture. These diagonals often contain figures that seem to support, or at least to converge on, a central field – a decorative device that would make better sense on a vault, where such figures would genuinely appear to be rising upwards towards the crown. The notion of supporting figures is stated more force-fully on those pavements where snake-legged Giants or fish-tailed Tritons occupy the spandrels of a design consisting of a large circular field set in a square. These figures, which raise their arms to bear the weight of the circular field, can be seen as 'reflections' of *telamones* painted or modelled or worked in mosaic upon the pendentives of a domed ceiling. In one

54, 30

91

British example, which formed part of the same pavement as the chariot-race from Horkstow, the backgrounds of the fields were rendered in red or blue rather than the more normal white of floor mosaics – a feature which strongly suggests the influence of ceiling decorations.

It is possible that other pavement designs, too, were inspired by vaults and their decorations. The familiar composition in which a central roundel is flanked by semicircles, with quadrants in the corners, for example, has sometimes been linked with domed ceilings. Where the quadrants are occupied by shells, the visual reference is strengthened, since a stucco shell was a familiar motif for the decoration of the semi-domes of apses or curved niches. So, too, the scheme of sprawling plants growing across the pavement from a root-stock in each corner could be based on types of ceiling decoration. Overall vines and the like are attested in both painted and mosaic wall decorations, for example on the vault of the little mausoleum M in the Vatican necropolis. They would have given the occupants of a room something of the impression of being under a leafy arbour.

Even if floor mosaics borrowed design elements from vaults and domes, this does not mean that they ever directly reflected the treatment of a vault or dome that actually existed in the same room. In the few instances where details of the vault decoration that accompanied a mosaic pavement are known, they invariably show a different design, complementary rather than reflective. Most pavements, in any case, employed schemes which are not indebted to vault designs at all. Where a debt exists, it is probable that the floor mosaicists treated vault designs merely as part of a general decorative repertory from which ideas were drawn. Interestingly, a few ceiling decorations illustrate a reverse trend of influence, borrowing their designs from pavements. The favourite mosaic pattern of eight-lozenge stars alternating with squares, for example, was copied in a couple of painted ceilings at Pompeii, though with a black-ground colour scheme alien to mosaics.

From considering general exchanges between mosaic and other media we may go on to look at relationships within a room. Although the evidence is obviously very limited, there are plenty of examples of decorative ensembles where a mosaic pavement was designed to take account of the wall and ceiling decorations with which it was combined. Many of the décors of Roman Italy, for example, seem to have been planned with a colour balance in mind. The black and white pavements, whether geometric or figured, provide a perfect foil to the polychromy of the wall paintings, and are often mirrored by all-white stucco relief or white-ground paintings on the ceiling (though in the grander rooms the polychromy of the walls is sometimes carried up on to the ceiling). A similar balance characterises the use of figural elements. In the period of the Pompeian First Style, wall decorations were largely composed of imitation blockwork, with only occasional use of figure scenes in narrow friezes set at eye-level; the associated ceiling decorations, so far as we can judge, were also architectural in type, with wooden panelling or stucco imitations thereof; the main figural emphasis was therefore reserved for the pavement, whose decoration was focused on a pictorial *emblema*. In the period of the Second Style, the emergence of illusionistic wall paintings, at first architectural but ultimately containing figures and figure scenes, was accompanied by a dramatic simplification of mosaic pavements, from which pictorial *emblemata* were rapidly eliminated, to be replaced by simple abstract or geometric treatments. Even when figural work eventually reappeared in pavements, it was usually of the black silhouette type which did not distract unduly from the *trompe l'oeil* architecture of the walls. In later times, with the triumph of polychrome figure work in western mosaics, something of the balance of earlier ensembles was lost, but even now the spreading of the figures across the surface, the use of geometric frameworks, the restricted range of colours and the predominance of a neutral white ground, all gave the pavements a lighter and more 'abstract' quality than the wall paintings with which they were combined.

Mosaic pavements are often linked to wall paintings by direct visual references. Dominant elements in the pavement sometimes lead the eye towards dominant elements in the wall decoration. In the Second Style, for example, the strip of mosaic ornament which marks off the actual *triclinium* zone from the forepart of a dining-room is often picked up by prominent painted pilasters on the side walls; these divide the painted decoration into different schemes, one more elaborate and richly coloured than the other. Sometimes there are particular patterns or motifs in the pavements which are echoed on the walls. In the early Second Style House of the Griffins in Rome, the pattern of perspective cubes (here rendered in *opus sectile*) in the central *emblema* of the pavement is repeated in painted form within the fictive architecture in the murals (where it perhaps reproduced actual sectile elements applied to the walls of Hellenistic palaces). More generally, there can be links in subject-matter. A representation of Venus in the pavement, for example, could be accompanied by scenes from mythical love stories on the walls. In baths, the marine creatures depicted on pavements sometimes recurred in the wall decoration (for example, at Münsingen in Switzerland).

In looking at the context of mosaics it is easy to forget another factor in the equation: the room's furnishings. Because these rarely survive we tend to treat the embellishment of architectural surfaces as an isolated phenomenon; but each room would have had its beds and couches (the position of which can sometimes, as we have seen, be determined from indications in the floor or wall decoration), its chests, cupboards, chairs, stools or tables. These in turn would have been adorned with cushions or drapes, the colours and themes of which may have been chosen to fit the surroundings. To these must be added the curtains that sometimes screened doorways and other openings. A conception of how the furniture and draperies contributed to the overall décor is offered by the interior settings shown in works of art, especially mythological paintings; but it is generally impossible to visualise the contents of spaces in real architectural contexts. An important element is thus missing from our assessment of a room's visual impact.

There are, of course, many ensembles where the links between pavements and murals are unclear or even totally lacking. Sometimes this is due to a partial redecoration, usually the replacement of wall paintings, which has produced juxtapositions unintended by the original decorators. Sometimes it is a case of a lack of interest in the idea of a planned ensemble – an *ad hoc* approach in which mosaicists and painters did not take great account of each others' contributions. This raises the more general questions of how craftsmen were organised, what relationships existed between them and the patrons, and how particular designs and themes were chosen. These are big and hardly answerable questions, and only a few tentative observations can be offered here.

While it is possible that the same craftsmen occasionally carried out both paintings and mosaics, the very different skills involved would normally have led to specialisation. There were certainly *pictores* ('painters') involved in mosaic production, as we know from inscriptions on pavements which distinguish between an artist who 'painted' and a craftsman who laid the tesserae; but painting here must refer to the creation of the cartoons from which the *tessellarii* worked. The *pictores* were the designers, and presumably often the skilled figure-workers, attached to firms of mosaicists. It was when such skilled designers were unavailable that some of the more bizarre efforts at figure depiction took place. A mosaicist who boasted at a site in Tunisia that he had carried out figure work 'without a painter' effectively demonstrated by his workmanship why a 'painter' was necessary!

In the organisation of mosaic production there were clearly many different possibilities. Firms regularly carrying out figure work may have consisted of one or more *pictores*, who were presumably the master craftsmen, assisted by lesser craftsmen and apprentices who did the routine work, copying the models, executing the geometric elements, or simply laying the background. Other firms may have specialised in geometric

92

92 *Venus pavement from Rudston (North Humberside, Britain). This crudely executed pavement of the second half of the fourth century shows how craftsmen sometimes lacked the skill to execute the classical schemes demanded by clients. Figures of beasts and* venatores *from the amphitheatre are combined with a central scene of Venus (goddess of love and beauty) and a Triton. Hull and East Riding Museum.*

work alone, hiring freelance *pictores* when required (such may have been the case with a mosaic in Spain where the *pictor* and the workshop owner were separate people). Alternatively, it would have been possible to buy ready-made *emblemata*. The size of firms clearly varied, and no doubt there was some movement of craftsmen between one firm and another. Large commissions, such as the villa at Piazza Armerina, would have involved firms taking on additional labour, or indeed different firms being called in to operate side by side. In laying a single pavement the number of individual craftsmen would naturally be conditioned by the size of the room and the amount of time available. Recent analysis of some of the geometric pavements at Piazza Armerina has suggested that the number of hands at work varied from two in small rooms to five in a medium-sized room and seven in the main peristyle. Probably the average firm in a small provincial city consisted of only two to four people, but the situation must have been very fluid. The continued existence of any firm would depend upon a steady supply of commissions, and the evidence from certain parts of the Roman Empire suggests strong fluctuations in demand, even periods in which production virtually ceased. In these circumstances mosaicists would often have had to move from place to place to secure work. That this happened is demonstrated not only by the transmission of patterns and motifs from one region to another (from northern Italy to the Rhône valley, for example, and from there to northern France and Switzerland) but also by information recorded in inscriptions. The signature on the

93 Lillebonne mosaic shows that the master craftsman was an Italian from Puteoli, while the epitaph of a mosaicist from Perinthus on the Black Sea states specifically that he had worked in many cities.

About the pay and status of ancient mosaicists we know very little. The presence of signatures upon several mosaics of the Roman period suggests that the craftsmen felt pride in their work, and some of the fine pictorial pieces of the Hellenistic period, at least six of which are signed, were productions of considerable technical virtuosity. But the figures given in

93 Hunting mosaic from
Lillebonne in northern
France, now in Rouen
(Museum of Antiquities).
The inscription in the
central panel indicates
that the mosaic was laid
by a mosaicist from
Puteoli in Italy with the
assistance (according to
the most likely
interpretation) of a local
apprentice named Amor.

Diocletian's price-fixing edict of AD 301 imply that, at that date at least, mosaicists were regarded as craftsmen of second rank, with rates of pay that compared unfavourably with others in the visual arts. While the income of the more highly esteemed mosaic specialist, the *musearius*, was fixed at a maximum of 60 denarii per day (plus keep), the wall-painter could earn up to 75 denarii and the figure-painter 150. The figure-modeller (*plastes imaginarius*), too, was rated higher than the *musearius*, earning up to 75 denarii. The *tessellarius* was allowed only 50 denarii, the same as a builder, a joiner, a baker or a blacksmith; of craftsmen in the decorative arts only the 'remaining workers in plaster' (probably those engaged in the mechanical task of making plaster casts of statues, statuettes and ornaments) earned as little as this. Nonetheless, it was evidently possible for successful mosaicists to accumulate considerable wealth and honours. In the second century P. Aelius Proclus, the son and successor of the mosaicist from Perinthus mentioned above, financed the decoration of a sanctuary of Tyche (Fortune) from his own pocket and was honoured by the erection of a public statue and by election to the city council. The potential rewards clearly varied. So too did mosaicists' legal status. While most were clearly of free birth, some were not. At least two signatures record servile status, and in other cases such status can be deduced from the form of the name or from the context. The slaves in question belonged either to a community or to individual masters, but we have no means of telling why they were employed on particular projects – whether they were working directly for their owners or were leased out to others, and, if they were working for their owners, whether these owners were producers or recipients of the mosaics.

Each firm of mosaicists clearly developed a particular range of compositions and figure subjects, not to mention 'trademark' details, which enable modern art-historians to identify broad groupings of related works and thus to trace certain patterns of transmission. But, for all the similarities between the works of a single firm, there are remarkably few pavements which can be regarded as anywhere near identical. The number of variations admitted, both within the basic schemes and in the choice and distribution of the motifs, seems almost infinite. No doubt the particular arrangements used in any room were chosen by the master craftsman in consultation with the client, who would have been shown a pattern-book with more or less detailed drawings of the firm's standard selection. Alternatively, the patron may have issued written specifications like those recorded on the Hellenistic papyrus from Egypt mentioned in Chapter 1: here, for a simple circular pavement with a central rosette enclosed by ornamental borders, all that the mosaicist needed to know was the type of ornaments, their arrangement and measurements. The rest was left to his knowledge of standard motifs and procedures. But, whatever the methods of specification in a given case, there was clearly enough flexibility for innumerable variations, often embodying the personal touch and taste of the craftsman, to emerge.

The motives which inspired a patron to choose particular designs and subjects were doubtless complex and varied. In recent years much discussion has centred on the possible presence of religious and intellectual programmes within figured mosaics; but, except where the choice of subjects is clearly ideological (as in Christian churches) or philosophical (as in certain pavements in the East) or idiosyncratic (as in a mysterious fourth-century pavement at Trier with an unusual mythological subject and what appears to be a cult-scene), it is difficult to prove symbolic intent. The use of mythological subjects alone does not indicate religious belief, because such subjects had become largely conventional. The vast majority of figure subjects comes from a widely available repertoire, and there is no *a priori* reason to believe that choices were not usually based upon banal and non-significant criteria, such as a personal fondness for certain mythical stories and for the literature in which these stories were told, an interest in particular activities and entertainments, such as hunting and chariot-racing, or simply the range of options offered by the local mosaicists'

94

94 *Ritual scene on a mosaic from Trier (late fourth century AD). The precise meaning is unclear, but Qodvoldeus and his assistants are probably engaged in a ceremony connected with a little-known cult to whose chapel the pavement belonged; it is thus one of the rare examples of a commission where mosaicists were not able to draw from the standard repertoire.*

pattern-books. In some cases the choice of subjects may have been determined partly by the number of fields available: a nine-compartment scheme lent itself to the Muses, a seven-compartment one to the planetary gods, and four corner fields to the Seasons or the Winds.

Obviously, once laid, the mosaics would have been seen and discussed by different viewers, each of whom would have put his or her own construction upon them, perhaps trying to find common messages in a set of disparate figure scenes much as the narrator in Petronius' novel *The Satyricon* searched for a meaning in three old masters juxtaposed in a picture gallery. But in most cases it is dangerous to read too much into a patron's intentions in commissioning a pavement. He would have been motivated by a desire to beautify his house, to satisfy his love of classical culture, to display his learning to guests and visitors – but not necessarily more than this.

We, too, can appreciate ancient mosaics in similar ways. They are colourful and attractive, and they appeal to our educated taste for the world of classical literature and thought. At the same time, they now have a historical dimension; they are invaluable documents of ancient life. Since we have very few written sources on the daily life of Greek and Roman households, archaeological discoveries relating to the domestic environment give us a remarkable insight into an aspect of the classical world that would otherwise be largely hidden from us. Among these discoveries ancient mosaics occupy a unique position. They are both works of art to be appreciated in their own right and vehicles which convey something of the concerns and aspirations of the people who lived with them. It is for these reasons that they exercise such an abiding interest for the modern world.

95 Dolphins confronted across a trident. Panel from the border of a calendar mosaic at Carthage, sections of which were lifted in 1857 and brought to the British Museum. Second half of the fourth century AD.

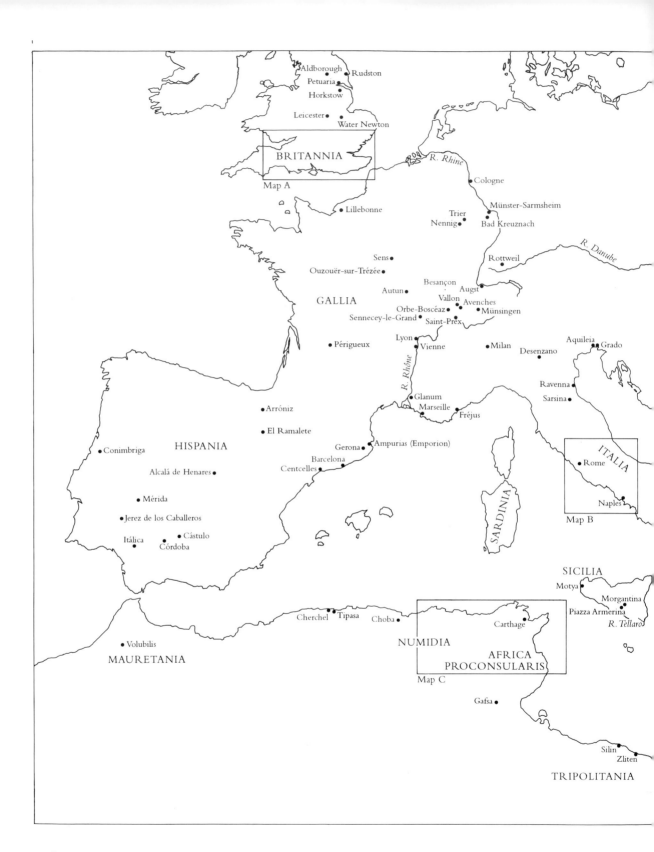

BRITANNIA

Aldborough
Rudston
Petuaria
Horkstow
Leicester
Water Newton

Map A

R. Rhine

Cologne

Münster-Sarmsheim
Lillebonne
Trier
Nennig
Bad Kreuznach

R. Danube

Rottweil

Sens
Ouzouër-sur-Trézée
Besançon
Autun
Augst
Vallon
Avenches
Orbe-Boscéaz
Münsingen
Sennecey-le-Grand
Saint-Prex

GALLIA

Lyon
Vienne
Milan
Desenzano
Aquileia
Grado

Périgueux

R. Rhône

Ravenna
Sarsina

Glanum
Marseille
Fréjus

Arróniz

El Ramalete

ITALIA

Rome

HISPANIA

Conimbriga

Gerona
Ampurias (Emporion)
Barcelona
Centcelles

Alcalá de Henares

Mérida

Jerez de los Caballeros

Itálica
Córdoba
Cástulo

SARDINIA

Map B

Naples

SICILIA

Motya
Morgantina
Piazza Armerina
R. Tellaro

Volubilis

MAURETANIA

Cherchel
Tipasa
Choba
Carthage

NUMIDIA

AFRICA
PROCONSULARIS

Gafsa

Map C

Silin
Zliten

TRIPOLITANIA

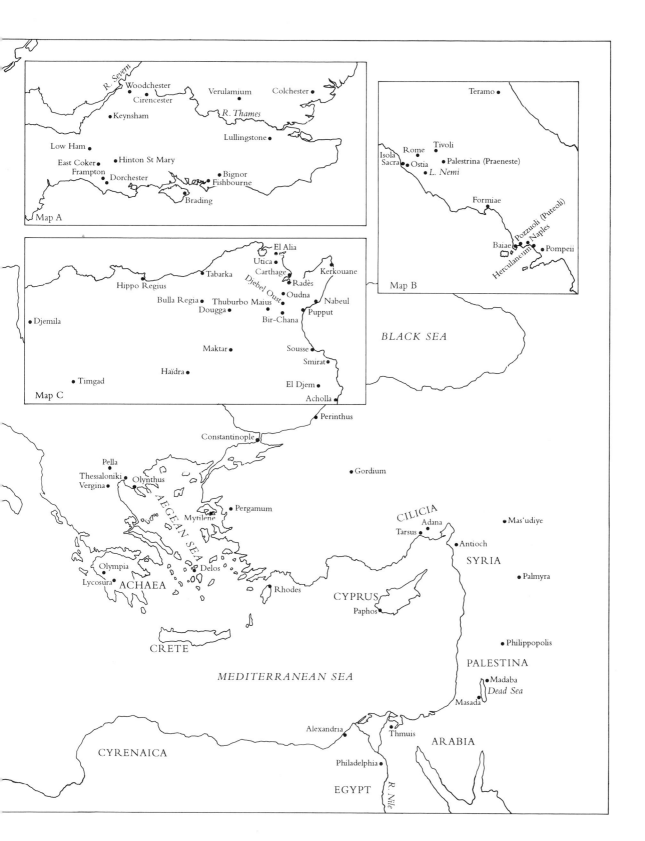

Map A

• Woodchester
R. Severn
• Cirencester
• Verulamium
• Colchester
• Keynsham
R. Thames
• Lullingstone
• Low Ham
• Hinton St Mary
• East Coker
• Frampton
• Dorchester
• Bignor
• Fishbourne
• Brading

Map B

• Teramo
• Rome
• Tivoli
Isola
Sacra
• Ostia
• Palestrina (Praeneste)
• L. Nemi
• Formiae
Pozzuoli (Puteoli)
• Naples
Baiae
Herculaneum
• Pompeii

Map C

• El Alia
• Utica
• Carthage
• Kerkouane
• Tabarka
• Radès
Djebel Oust
• Hippo Regius
• Oudna
• Bulla Regia
• Thuburbo Maius
• Nabeul
• Dougga
• Pupput
• Bir-Chana
• Djemila
• Maktar
• Sousse
• Smirat
• Timgad
• Haïdra
• El Djem
• Acholla

BLACK SEA

• Perinthus

• Constantinople

• Pella
• Thessaloniki
• Olynthus
• Vergina
• Gordium
• Pergamum
AEGEAN
• Mytilene
SEA
CILICIA
• Adana
• Mas'udiye
• Tarsus
• Antioch
• Olympia
• Delos
SYRIA
• Lycosura
ACHAEA
• Palmyra
• Rhodes
CYPRUS
CRETE
• Paphos
• Philippopolis
MEDITERRANEAN SEA
PALESTINA
• Madaba
Dead Sea
• Masada
• Alexandria
• Thmuis
ARABIA
CYRENAICA
• Philadelphia
EGYPT
R. Nile

GLOSSARY

Bacchante   Female devotee of the god Dionysus (Bacchus)

Candelabrum   Lampstand; decorative motif of similar form

Chip mosaic   Mosaic formed of irregular chippings of stone, generally white

Coffer   Recessed panel in a wooden, stone or stucco ceiling

Corpus (-ora)   Detailed publication in the form of a systematic catalogue

Crenellation   Motif imitating the crenellations of a fortification wall, frequently used in the borders of mosaic pavements

Cupid   Winged love-god (Roman equivalent of the Greek god Eros), usually in the form of an infant

Dentils   Series of tooth-like projections, used especially of hanging blocks found in Greek architecture

Emblema (-ata)   Literally '(something) inserted'; used especially of a mosaic panel prepared separately and inserted into a pavement the rest of which was laid on the spot

Eros (-otes)   See Cupid

Exedra   Open-fronted recess in a *gymnasium* or house, found especially behind the porticoes of peristyles

Guilloche   Decorative border in the form of various kinds of braid or plait

Gymnasium   Greek public building designed initially for the military training of young men but increasingly associated with physical and intellectual training in general

Lozenge   Diamond shape; rhombus

Lithostroton   'Strewn stone', commonly used of a decorative paving with small irregular pieces of stone, often in different colours

Meander   Decorative motif like a labyrinth, consisting of lines turning in and out at right angles and crossing one another

Musearius   Craftsman who specialised in *(opus) museum* or *musivum*

Museum   Literally 'pertaining to the Muses'; used (because the art-form began in grottoes sacred to the nymphs or the Muses) to signify wall mosaic

Musivarius   See *musearius*

Musivum   See *museum*

Nucleus   Upper layer of mortar in the bedding for a mosaic pavement

Nymph   Female spirit inhabiting water, sea, woods, etc.

Nymphaeum (-a)   Decorative fountain, derived from grottoes and similar structures sacred to the nymphs

Oecus (-i)   Large reception room or salon in a Hellenistic or Roman house

Opus   'Work', used (mainly by modern writers) with various adjectives to describe craftwork techniques

Palmette   Decorative motif in the form of a stylised palm-leaf

Pelta (-ae)   Decorative motif in the form of the shield carried by Amazons (mythical female warriors), crescent-shaped with one or two curving recesses cut in the upper edge

Pendentive	In architecture the triangular portion of a sphere which, in a square or polygonal room, effects the transition from the angles of the walls to a circular dome	*Statumen*	Layer of rubble underneath the mortar bedding for a mosaic pavement
Peristyle	Colonnaded court (or garden) found in *gymnasia* and houses	Stucco	Fine lime-plaster used for decorative surfacing and work in relief
Pointillism	Technique of painting with juxtaposed dots of different colours, associated with Georges Seurat and other painters of the late nineteenth century	*Telamon (-ones)*	Architectural support in the form of a male figure
		Terracotta	Baked clay, the material of pottery, tiles and bricks
Psyche	The soul; often depicted in Roman art as a child with butterfly wings, the female companion of Cupid	*Terrazzo*	Modern Italian term for various forms of mortar or cement paving containing stone chippings
Rainbow style	Style of mosaic in which the colours of tesserae are arranged in diagonal sequence rather than in rows	*Tessellarius*	Craftsman who specialised in *(opus) tessellatum*
		Tessellatum	'Tessellated'; commonly used in the phrase *opus tessellatum* to distinguish floor mosaic from wall mosaic and from *opus sectile*
Rosette	Decorative motif in the form of a flower with radiating petals	Tessera (-ae)	Cube of stone, glass or terracotta used in the making of a mosaic
Rudus	Lower layer of mortar in the bedding for a mosaic pavement	*Tesserarius*	See *tessellarius*
Satyr	Half-bestial woodland spirit, one of the circle of the god Dionysus	*Triclinium (-a)*	Arrangement of three couches found in a Roman dining-room; by extension, the dining-room itself
Sectile	Literally 'cut'; commonly used in the phrase *opus sectile* to signify a surface decoration obtained by cutting pieces of stone to special geometric or other shapes		
		Trompe l'oeil	Form of artistic representation which produces an illusion of reality so as to 'deceive the eye'
Signinum	Waterproof mortar containing an aggregate of crushed terracotta, so called after the Italian city of Signia (Segni) in which the technique is said to have been invented	*Vermiculatum*	Literally 'worm-like', commonly used to describe the technique of pictorial mosaics made with minute tesserae (perhaps because the tesserae appear to form sinuous curves within the picture)
Spandrel	Triangular space above the haunches of an arch; similar space between a circle and the angles of an enclosing square	Wave-crest	Decorative border formed by a continuous series of hooks resembling the crests of waves

SELECT BIBLIOGRAPHY

General

H.P. L'Orange and P.J. Nordhagen, *Mosaics*, London 1966

D.J. Smith, 'Mosaics', in M. Henig (ed.), *A Handbook of Roman Art*, Oxford 1983, pp. 116-38

C. Balmelle *et al.*, *Le décor géométrique de la mosaïque romaine. Répertoire graphique et descriptif des compositions linéaires et isotropes*, Paris 1985

C. Bertelli (ed.), *Mosaics*, New York 1988, pp. 9-44

K.M.D. Dunbabin, *A History of Ancient Mosaics*, Cambridge, forthcoming

Collections of essays

La mosaïque gréco-romaine (Colloque international, Paris 29 août-3 septembre 1963), Paris 1965

La mosaïque gréco-romaine ii (IIe colloque international pour l'étude de la mosaïque antique, Vienne 30 août-4 septembre 1971), Paris 1971

Mosaïque: recueil d'hommages à Henri Stern, Paris 1983

R. Farioli Campanati (ed.), *III Colloquio internazionale sul mosaico antico Ravenna 6-10 settembre 1980*, Ravenna 1984

J.-P. Darmon and A. Rebourg (eds), *La mosaïque gréco-romaine* iv (IVe colloque international pour l'étude de la mosaïque antique, Trèves 8-14 août 1984), Paris 1994

P. Johnson, R. Ling and D.J. Smith (eds), *Fifth International Colloquium on Ancient Mosaics held at Bath, England, on September 5-12, 1987 (Journal of Roman Archaeology*, Supplementary Series 9), vol. i, Ann Arbor 1994; vol. ii, Ann Arbor 1995

Technique

F. Sear, 'Wall and vault mosaics', in D. Strong and D. Brown (eds), *Roman Crafts*, London 1976, pp. 231-9

D.S. Neal, 'Floor mosaics', in Strong and Brown (op. cit.), pp. 241-52

M. Donderer, *Die Mosaizisten der Antike und ihre wirtschaftliche und soziale Stellung. Eine Quellenstudie*, Erlangen 1989

Greek mosaics

C.M. Robertson, 'Greek mosaics', *Journal of Hellenic Studies* lxxxv (1965), pp. 72-89

C.M. Robertson, 'Greek mosaics: a postscript', *Journal of Hellenic Studies* lxxxvii (1967), pp. 133-5

K.M.D. Dunbabin, 'Technique and materials of Hellenistic mosaics', *American Journal of Archaeology* lxxxiii (1979), pp. 265-77

D. Salzmann, *Untersuchungen zu den antiken Kieselmosaiken*, Berlin 1982

Italy

M.E. Blake, 'The pavements of the Roman buildings of the Republic and early Empire', *Memoirs of the American Academy in Rome* viii (1930)

M.E. Blake, 'Roman mosaics of the second century in Italy', *Memoirs of the American Academy in Rome* xiii (1936), pp. 67-214

M.E. Blake, 'Mosaics of the late Empire in Rome and vicinity', *Memoirs of the American Academy in Rome* xvii (1940), pp. 81-130

J.R. Clarke, *Roman Black-and-White Figural Mosaics*, New York 1979

M. Donderer, *Die Chronologie der römischen Mosaiken in Venetien und Istrien bis zur Zeit der Antonine*, Berlin 1986

The East

D. Levi, *Antioch Mosaic Pavements*, Princeton 1947

J. Balty, 'La mosaïque en Proche-Orient, I. Des origines à la Tétrarchie', in *Aufstieg und Niedergang der römischen Welt* ii.12.2 (1981), pp. 347-429

D. Michaelides, *Cypriot Mosaics*, Nicosia 1987

S. Campbell, *The Mosaics of Antioch*, Toronto 1988

Northern and western provinces

Recueil général des mosaïques de la Gaule, Paris 1957-

K. Parlasca, *Die römischen Mosaiken in Deutschland*, Berlin 1959

V. von Gonzenbach, *Die römischen Mosaiken der Schweiz*, Basel 1961

A. Kiss, *Roman Mosaics in Hungary*, Budapest 1973

Corpus de mosaicos de España, Madrid 1978-

J.-P. Darmon, 'Les mosaïques en Occident, I', *Aufstieg und Niedergang der römischen Welt* ii.12.2 (1981), pp. 266-319

W. Jobst, *Antike Mosaikkunst in Österreich*, Vienna 1985

Britain

D.S. Neal, *Roman Mosaics in Britain* (*Britannia* Monograph Series I), London 1981

P. Johnson, *Romano-British Mosaics* (Shire Archaeology 25), Princes Risborough 1982

R. Ling, 'Mosaics in Roman Britain: discoveries and research since 1945', *Britannia* xxviii (1997), pp. 259-95

North Africa

Corpus des mosaïques de Tunisie, Tunis 1973-

K.M.D. Dunbabin, *The Mosaics of Roman North Africa*, Oxford 1978

M. Blanchard *et al.*, *Roman Mosaics from North Africa. Floor Mosaics from Tunisia*, London and New York 1996

Wall and vault mosaics

F.B. Sear, *Roman Wall and Vault Mosaics* (*Mitteilungen des Deutschen Archäologischen Instituts. Römische Abteilung*, Ergänzungsheft 23), Heidelberg 1977

ILLUSTRATION ACKNOWLEDGMENTS

A. Almazán (courtesy of Janine Lancha): 52. Anderson, Rome (12825): 78. Archaeological Receipts Fund, Athens: 11, 12. Baltimore Museum of Art, Antioch Subscription Fund (mosaic BMA 1937.129): 90. Alix Barbet: 13. Bardo Museum, Tunis: 64. Bridgeman Art Library, London/New York (KAB 76949): 77. © Copyright The British Museum: front cover (GR Mosaic 25), back cover (GR Mosaic 54j), 44 (GR Mosaic 7), 47 (PRB 1965,4-9,1), 95 (GR Mosaic 29h). Centre Camille Jullian, CNRS, University of Provence: 55, 60, 91 (G. Réveillac, 48.795). Centre d'Etudes Alexandrines: half-title page, 14. Department of Antiquities, Cyprus: 89. Damascus Museum: 38. C.M. Dixon: 15. M. Donderer: 41. English Heritage Photographic Library: 85. Fibbi-Aeppli, Grandson, Switzerland: 51. E. Flatters: 48. Service Archéologique Cantonal, Fribourg: 8. German Archaeological Institute, Berlin (80.2.285): 24. German Archaeological Institute, Rome: 1 (54.38), 65 (61.514), 67 (64.737). Getty Research Institute, Research Library, Wim Swaan Photograph Collection: frontispiece, 2, 6. Giraudon, Paris: 34, 93. W.A. Graham, © Michael Larvey: 27, 30. Sonia Halliday Photographs: 7, 68 (F.H.C. Birch). G. Hellenkemper Salies: 42. Michael Holford: 5, 18, 75. Interdipress, Naples: 88. Michael Larvey: 26. L.A. Ling: 74. L.A. and R.J. Ling: 21. R.J. Ling: 3, 4, 9, 19, 20, 28, 29, 31, 32, 43, 46, 49, 50, 54, 56, 57, 59, 61, 72, 82, 86, 87, 92. University of Manchester, Department of Art History and Archaeology: 23. Leonard von Matt: 16, 17, 25. Gilles Mermet: 58, 62, 63, 66. Museo Nacional de Arte Romano, Mérida: 53. University of Pennsylvania Museum, Philadelphia (77894; drawing J. Last and C. Polykarpou): 10. M. Piccirillo: 70, 71. Polish Archaeological Mission, Paphos (courtesy of Wiktor A. Daszewski): 39. Princeton University, Art Museum, Gift of the American Committee for the Excavation of Antioch and Vicinity, 1939: 36. Princeton University, Department of Art and Archaeology, Antioch Archive: 35, 37, 40. Rheinisches Landesmuseum, Trier (Thomas Zühmer): 94. St Andrews University Library (MS 36966, reproduced by permission of The Walker Trust): 69. Archivio Fotografico di San Pietro in Vaticano, Rome: 76. Scala: 73, 79, 80. Vatican Museums (A. Bracchetti): 22. Paul Veysseyre: 45. Warburg Institute, London: 81. Catherine Wood: 83, 84. Worcester Art Museum, Worcester, Mass.: 33. Map by Elizabeth Errington.

INDEX